A R T & R E A L I T Y

The Standard

Reference Guide and Business Plan

For Actively
Developing Your Career
As An Artist

Robert J. Abbott
Catherine Newman

Library of Congress Catalog Number: 93-71486

ISBN 0-9636474-0-7

This book may be purchased for educational, business, or sales promotional use. For information, please write or call:

The Contemporary Marketing Group
1345 Coral Drive
Laguna Beach, CA 92663

(714) 497-6052 Telephone
(714) 497-0471 Facsimile

FIRST EDITION

TABLE OF CONTENTS

PREFACE

If you are happy with your art work but frustrated by the business side of the art world, or if you feel you have a great product but are the only one who knows it, then it is time to change your strategy. This book was conceived to meet the needs of the artist and artisan wishing to develop a successful career; the self-taught artist as well as the graduate from a top university. The methods and information provided in this book are applicable not only to the avant garde artist but to the amateur artist as well.

A wide chasm exists between the artists and their work, and the galleries, museums, and other exhibition spaces. This great expanse has been created by the inability of artists to present their works effectively to qualified galleries, museums, and other venues that can help advance their careers. The lack of understanding by both the artist and the art world regarding how to communicate each other's needs effectively, has left many artists out in the cold. This book was created to fill this void, and to help bring artists to the highest level of success they are capable of attaining in the shortest period of time.

Whether your goal is a show at the local gallery or an exhibition at the Museum of Modern Art, knowing where you have been, where you are now, and where you want to go is imperative. Planning your career path as an artist, as for any profession, will bring you a greater probability of attaining the success you so desire. You must understand the workings of the art world-the rules by which you "play the game."

Once you know the ***who, what, when, where, why,*** and especially ***how*** to get your work out there, you can plan a strategy and build your career. Having knowledge and focus will eliminate speculation, confusion, and costly mistakes which can rob artists of their careers. Many of the "secrets" not shared by the art world are unveiled for you. Thousands of dollars of money-saving tips and techniques are laid out for you to use. You will develop the knowledge to recognize and take advantage of those opportunities that present themselves to you.

The methods presented in this book are the result of years of firsthand experience with the frustration and determination involved in drawing an artist's work out of the studio and into the public arena. As director of the Modern Museum of Art in Southern California, I was bombarded by artists seeking to exhibit their work and find representation. The interaction between a director, curator, or dealer and the artist often comes down to the effectiveness of the artist's portfolio. Although I saw hundreds of presentations, the majority were at best mediocre, and only a handful truly caught my eye. I began to see clearly what made the difference between success and failure. This book was created to set the standard of presentation by which the art world measures the artist's work.

Robert J. Abbott

HOW TO USE THIS BOOK

This book is designed to actively guide you step-by-step through the process of developing and executing your own career plan. Rather than just hitting you with a lot of information, this guide walks you gently through each stage of the process.

The best way to use this book is to take it one chapter at a time, starting at the very beginning with the Artist Evaluation. The evaluation will give you the opportunity to get your bearings and determine where you presently are. Armed with this knowledge, you will begin to progress forward through the book and into your career. The chapter "Planning Strategies" will give you an overview of the steps towards actively building your plan and career. An appendix listing of other suggested readings on each of the various topics discussed in this book has been provided for your reference. Many of these resources are available at your local or university libraries.

This book is not a passive book. It is designed to be worked in and referenced on an ongoing basis during your career. Specific chapters refer to "Career Plan" worksheets relating to the focus of that chapter. Samples have been completed within this book to show you what information or action to look for and how to find it. Clean copies of the worksheets are provided separately at the back of the binder for you to copy and use as you need. It is advisable to keep a clean, master copy of each worksheet and to use photocopies for your work.

As you complete each chapter and the corresponding worksheets, insert the sheet(s) behind the divider referring to the current topic. You will be gradually building your career plan. Remove this reference guide from the binder if you find you do not have enough room for your work as you progress. With time, your plan will grow as will your career.

ABOUT THE AUTHORS

Robert J. Abbott

Author and noted lecturer, Robert Abbott believes education and planning are the keys to success for any artist. "Educating yourself about the art community, its intricacies, and idiosyncracies are the keys to any artist's success. You must understand the needs of the people you are approaching, how to present your work to these people, and how your work can succeed within their gallery, museum or other venue. There are so many diverse aspects of the art community open to the knowledgeable artist. Success is attainable."

Abbott is no stranger to success within the art community. As director of the Modern Museum of Art, he established himself as a member of the institutional community. He developed not only a recognized museum but also the nation's leading educational outreach program, as recognized by the U.S. Department of Education. Abbott has taken the seemingly impenetrable world of art, with all its complexities, and politics, and has broken it down to its basic principles; what it takes to make it in the business of art.

As past president of the fine art publishing firm, Fine Art Communication Technologies, Abbott developed the publishing careers of numerous artists. "There are many ways to publish your work, even on a modest budget. Once again, the key is educating yourself to your options, and what will work for you."

Abbott is testimony to the successes of planning through establishing his own career as a fine artist. "The keys to growth as an artist are the careful, step-by-step planning of your career path. Each exhibition has a purpose, leading to the next goal within the plan." Abbott's own plan, and execution of his plan shows you that any artist who plans their career path, and focuses their efforts in the direction of that planned path can attain their goals, be they financial or academic success.

Art & Reality -- The Standard Reference Guide and Business Plan for Actively Developing Your Career as an Artist, is one of Abbott's most recent contributions to the art community. "***Art & Reality*** is not merely a 'how-to' book, but is a complete career guide for the individual artist. Whether you are a well seasoned artist or just starting out, ***Art & Reality*** is a ***must do*** for every artist who is serious about a future and career!"

Catherine Newman also believes that knowledge, planning and focus are the keys to an artist's success. "You must have a clear understanding of your goals; what it is you wish to achieve with your art. Armed with this and an awareness of the needs and goals of the people you wish to approach with your work, you will have far greater opportunities for success."

As founder and former vice president of a national marketing design firm, Newman brings to the artist many techniques for organizing and marketing their works to meet their own aspirations. "An artist is often not comfortable with promoting him- or herself to the public. Many would prefer to work with their art and leave the presentations and promotions to someone else. ***Art & Reality*** shows the artist how easy planning and developing a successful career can be."

Art & Reality -- The Standard Reference Guide and Business Plan for Actively Developing Your Career as an Artist, gives the artist the power to successfully draw their art out of the studio and into the public's eye. "***Art & Reality*** is a must do for all artists, the veteran and the novice. There are many levels to the art world to which all types of art have a purpose and an application. ***Art & Reality*** guides the artist in finding a welcome place within the art world."

ANALYSIS
ARTIST EVALUATION SURVEY

The first step in developing a successful career plan for you as a professional artist is to clearly understand where you are starting from -- at what point are you in your career ***now***.

This survey asks you to clearly and concisely assess your present work. You will reflect on your activities to date, including the directions you have followed either voluntarily or involuntarily and the results they have produced. You will assess the quality of your education, whether it has helped you or how a lack of a current education has possibly hindered you. You will list the venues where your art has been shown. Finally, you will be asked to decide what you want your future to be; what makes making art worthwhile for you. These responses will be the foundation from which ***YOUR*** career plan will be developed.

Complete the Analysis Thoroughly and Honestly

We urge you to be ***honest*** with yourself. Set aside an hour or two to think about the questions being posed. Answer each question completely. Rambling, tangential answers will only serve to confuse you later in the process.

Review Your Answers

After you have completed the analysis, reread your answers critically. If you find there are areas you are not sure of, you may have discovered a point needing development. Throughout this book, we will point to areas such as this and suggest ways in which you can strengthen your knowledge or ability.

Decision in Direction

Together we will examine your responses, what they mean, and how they can be used to further your career, thus ultimately building ***YOUR*** career plan. Accompanied by action on your part, your plan can be used daily to achieve the results you deserve.

Never Be Discouraged

Whenever one scrutinizes oneself as microscopically as we will, you could have a tendency to become discouraged. ***Ignore it!*** You have made a decision to put your career on the right track by selecting this book. Be proud that you are taking control. Each artist is an individual who has a lot to offer in his or her own way.

ARTIST EVALUATION SURVEY

Artist Name: *Michelle Talvison* **Date:** *12 / 10/ 92*

Address: *1556 South Watkins Drive*

City: *Los Angeles* **State:** *CA* **Zip Code:** *90046*

Telephone: *(213) 555-1212* **Facsimile:** *(213) 555-2323*

Art

1. Describe your work.

   Abstract figurative - much of my work deals with social issues. Over the last three years my work has developed a strong continuity, both in my paintings and sculpture pieces.

2. Describe the style of your work.

   Again, I would say my works would probably be called abstract expressionism by most people - although I have my own unique style. Some people compare my work to Edward Munch and also Keifer. I tend to use the human figure in much of my work which seems to make it more accessible than pure abstraction.

3. How long have you worked in this style?

   I began working in this style about 5 years ago but it really began to come together 3 years ago. It has not changed a lot since that time, only matured in the same technique.

4. Has your style changed? Yes ___ No _✓_

5. Do you change your style frequently? Infrequently? Describe.

Not often over the past three years. Early in my career, I experimented on a regular basis. I seem to have found a style that works for me.

6. Describe the materials, media and general dimensions of your art.

I like to work with large canvases - anywhere from 48" square to 6' x 8'. I use oil and acrylic and often work with bronzes made from plasters. I use dark colors, often bleeding them for unusual imagery.

7. Briefly, what is your artistic philosophy?

To express my ideas in a gestural way - to allow the viewer a glimse into my ideas. I do this with imagery and color.

8. Where do you get your inspiration for works?

From everything around me - my daily experiences in life - particularly tensions in the world, the beauty of nature and man's inability to deal with one another.

9. Do you feel you have a good understanding of your philosophy?
Yes _✓_ No ___ Why?

I try to understand my subject matter to its fullest before I try to express them on canvas or in bronze. I do alot of reading and alot of studying. My goal is to alert others to the effects the subject matter has on their daily lives.

10. Do you feel others understand your philosophy?
Yes _✓_ No ___ Why?

I have had the opportunity to show my work in exhibitions where I have been able to talk to those attending. For the most part they see my message. They may not agree with it, but they understand what I am saying.

11. What other artists do you admire?

Jasper Johns, Pablo Picasso, Andy Warhol and many more. Georgia O'Keeffe and many more.

12. What inspires you about their work?

I like the freedom they seem to have in producing work - that they do or did what they wanted to do rather than being dictated to or controlled by other influences. I admire artists who have explored new boundaries or ideas such as Andy Warhol.

13. Compare your art to other artists in terms of style, quality, technique, and price.

I would say that my work is something like Jasper Johns and Andy Warhol - a combination of both. My technique has become pretty strong as I have been developing it now for 6 years. The quality is good - some pieces are stronger than others. My prices are not at all where I wish they were although in the area I live, they are above average.

14. Write a one-paragraph biography of yourself as an artist.

Born: New York City, 1959. I studied at New York University, graduating with an MFA in 1984. After graduation, I worked as a studio assistant for Anthony Michaels. Under his tutelage, I experimented with styles, media and expression of ideas. Two years later I began exhibiting a consistent body of works and lecturing to university students about my media techniques.

In the process of continuing my education, I have made contacts with educators from across the country, some of which who have helped me obtain exhibitions.

Market Survey

Understanding the possible marketplaces for your work is an important aspect of developing a successful career plan. Avenues through which you have had prior achievements may only be "the tip of the iceberg." With good planning and an open mind, you will discover other possible venues for your work.

15. Where do you feel your work best fits?

- ✓ Galleries
- ✓ Museums
- __ Art Fairs
- __ Retail Stores
- ✓ Other(s): *Colleges and Universities*

16. Does your art have a geographical influence, i.e., seascapes, etc.?

Not really - I would say it is universal in content and subject matter.

17. What geographical areas are your collectors from?

Primarily the East Coast / Metropolitan Areas - although I do have a few collectors from Europe.

18. Does your art appeal to the general public or to a more "art educated" sector? Please elaborate.

The art educated - as the work is quite colorful but the subject matter is "tough". I seem to sell to people who collect more than decorate.

19. What types of galleries have shown your work?

In the area in which I live, I show in the best galleries with recognized "on the edge" artists. These galleries show fine art of contemporary artists; paintings, sculptures and graphic pieces.

20. What types of museums have shown your work?

I have shown my work in two group museum shows. The museums focused on contemporary European artists but hold yearly shows for local artists.

21. What types of other places have shown your work?

I have had good results at colleges and universities. Shows in libraries, banks, art fairs, etc., have been difficult because of the agressive subject matter.

22. What price range has your art sold in?

a. Through Galleries *$600 - $2,200*
b. Through Your Studio *$100 - $2,200*
c. Through Art Fairs ____
d. Through Other Venues ____ ____

23. Has your art ever been published? (i.e., limited edition prints, etc.)
__ Self Published __ Publishing Company ✓ Never Published

24. What price range were the published works sold for? $ *N / A*

25. How many pieces were published in each edition? *N / A*

26. What method of printing was used to publish your work?

N / A

27. Were you satisfied with the results? Explain.

N / A - People frequently ask me if I have something in print. I feel I could offers something in a price range which is affordable to more people yet keep the integrity of what I have achieved price-wise to date.

28. If you have not been published, would you be interested in publishing your work?
✓ Yes __ No

Shows and Exhibitions

Provide a listing of all shows and exhibitions in which you have participated to date. Include **ANY** and **ALL** showings of your works, i.e., *location, dates, group or solo, works on display, coordinator of the event, etc.* If you have a current biography sheet already prepared, simply attach that to this section. If you are a new artist or have not shown your works extensively, do not be discouraged. You have wisely chosen to carefully plan your introduction to the art world.

29. Galleries/Commercial Spaces

*** I am only listing the last 3 years.*

1989 Time-Space Gallery, New York, NY - Group Show

1989 Coll Gallery, Chicago, IL - Group Show

1989 Roskins Gallery, Los Angeles, CA - Solo Exhibition

1990 Daniel James Gallery, San Jose, CA - Group Show

1990 Time-Space Gallery, New York, NY - Group Show

1991 Coll Gallery, Chicago, IL - Solo Exhibition

1992 LA Contemporary Arts, Los Angeles, CA - Group Show

30. Museums/Institutions

1992 Mockteller Museum, San Francisco, CA - Group Show

1992 Alternative Musuem, Los Angeles, CA - Group Show

31. Alternative Spaces

1992 New Arts Alternative Space, Chicago, IL - Group Show

1992 The Temporary Contemporary, Chicago, IL - Group Show

32. School Exhibitions

1990 Fine Arts Gallery, Lexington Art School, Lexington, KY - Group Show
1991 Alumni Exhibition, New York University, New York, NY - Group Show
1992 Alumni Exhibition, New York University, New York, NY - Group Show

33. Competitions

1992 Tri-State Arts Festival, Sacramento, CA - 2nd place - sculpture
1992 New England Fine Arts Council Competition, Boston, MA
- 1st place - sculpture

34. Public Spaces

N / A

35. Private Collections (For your use only)

Dr. & Mrs. Richard Elliott, Boston, MA
Mockteller Museum Collection, San Francisco, CA
Alternative Museum Collection, Los Angeles, CA
Thomas Coll Collection, Chicago, IL
New York University Alumni Collection, New York, NY

36. Art Fairs/Festivals

1991 Los Angeles Art Fair, Los Angeles, CA
1991 Miami Art Celebration, Miami, FL

37. Other(s)

N / A

38. Are you an active member of an arts organization? Museum? Describe.

Yes. I am a member of the Mockteller Museum Volunteer Guild - helping each year to organize the fund raising auction and the children's exhibition.

39. Are you involved in any community work relating to the arts? Describe.

Yes. I volunteer my services twice a month to a local mental health institution for resident art workshops. There is an uninhibited self-expression in their art which helps their treatment and my personal growth as an artist.

Education

Education can be an important facet in the development of your career as a professional artist. It helps you be aware of the evolution of art throughout the history of man, its influence on social values and perceptions of the times, and the power that individual artists have had on society. Education, either formal or informal, broadens you as an artist and contributes to your understanding of the realms and responsibilities of the artist. A formal education is not a requirement to becoming an artist, although keeping informed will help expand your opportunities.

40. What art education have your received? Include the dates and locations of high school, college, and continuing education as appropriate.

    1981 - 84 MFA - New York University, New York, NY
    1977 - 81 BA - California Arts College, Sacramento, CA
    1973 - 77 Sacramento High School, Sacramento, CA

41. Have you studied Art History or other art related courses? Please elaborate.

    Yes. Two years of Art History studies during MFA work. I explored the many periods of art and their influences upon and by society.

42. Have you interned with another artist or institution? Attended artist workshops?

    I was a studio assistant for Anthony Michaels. I try to attend workshops and lectures of artist whom I respect.

43. Do you visit the shows and exhibitions of other artists on a fairly regular basis?
    Yes _✓_ No ___

44. What types of education are you involved in at this time or plan to be in the near future?

    I attend workshops and lectures regularly. I am interested in applying for an artist-in-residency program abroad - Europe (Italy or France is my preference.)

Goals

45. What is your short term (6 month) goal for your art career?

1. To organize my work into a cohesive presentation
2. I would like to obtain my first actual dealer/representative
3. To apply for an artist-in-residency program
4. To publish a small limited edition of two pieces of my work

46. What is your 2 year goal?

1. To firmly establish myself in Southern California
2. To begin establishing myself in New York, aiming for Europe
3. To apply and receive an artist-in-residency grant in Europe

47. What is your 5 year goal?

1. To sell and show my works throughout the United States and Europe
2. To exhibit in a number of European museums
3. More museum shows in general

48. What is the ultimate achievement - the goal of all goals - for you as an artist?

To create work which is considered historically important by my peers and the art community.

49. Is selling your work a major factor to your art work?
Yes ✓ No ___ Why?

I have chosen art as my life-long career. I need to sell works to purchase more supplies to create more work. Teaching helps to presently supplement my income and keeps me in touch with the art community.

50. Are you willing to financially support expenses for developing your career, i.e., presentation materials, travel, etc.? ✓ Yes __ No

Productivity

51. How much time do you devote to your work?

    In a day? *3 - 4 hours*

    In a week? *18 - 25 hours*

52. How long, on an average, does it take to complete a piece?

    1 hour to 3 days depending upon the complexity of the piece

53. What percentage of your work product would you consider strong enough for exhibition in your chosen market?

    Approximately 75% - I only keep those pieces which I feel are strong

54. How prolific are you? How many pieces do you complete ...

    In a week? *1 - 2 paintings & 5 drawings*
    In a month? *3 - 6 paintings*
    In a year? *a lot if need be*

55. Are you able to support yourself through the sales of your works?
    Yes ✓ No ___

56. Are you employed at another job?
    Full Time ___ Part Time ✓ None ___

57. How many times a year do you present your work?

    To galleries? *3*
    To museums? *0*

58. Do you cold call on galleries? __ Yes ✓ No

59. Do you cold call on museums? __ Yes ✓ No

60. How many quality pieces do you presently have available for exhibition? *10*

61. How do you handle rejection?

    Fairly well - I frequently solicit opinions of my work from people who I respect.

Added Value for your Evaluation

This book is designed to guide you step by step through the process of developing and executing your own career plan as an artist. You will be selecting and developing your presentation materials, identifying prospective markets and opportunities and presenting your works to them. ***Let us help you develop your plan and presentation to achieve the greatest success possible for your career.***

As an added value to your commitment to success, the **Artist Evaluation Service** is provided to you to completely evaluate your work, your goals, the marketplaces and opportunities available to you, and the steps you can take to develop your career towards your goals. Send us your Artist Evaluation Survey along with either photographs or slides of your work. A complete constructive review of your art and your evaluation survey will be returned to you. We do not take a passive role in your career but rather, we actively help you to attain those goals which are important to you.

Or you may wish to send your presentation to us as if we are the gallery or museum you have targeted to present your work to. Prepare a complete presentation package following the guidelines provided in the chapter "Developing Your Presentation Materials." In turn, we will review your entire package recommending improvements and corrections if needed to help strengthen your presentation and your overall career plan. This service is provided to help you take control of your career without "stubbing your toe" on the first try.

Mail your evaluation and presentation materials to:

The Contemporary Marketing Group
1345 Coral Drive
Laguna Beach, CA 92651

Or call for further information:

(714) 497-6052

All evaluations and presentations must be accompanied with a completed Artist Registration Card and payment for the service fee as instructed on the registration card.

PLANNING STRATEGIES

The particular strategies you choose in building your career will vary according to your individual objectives and certainly may change as your plan is set into motion. Although each step must then be implemented in a timely, organized manner, only your flexibility and patience can ensure that minor stumbling blocks do not become major obstacles in your career path. Equipped with general awareness of what is expected of you, you will find such problems the exception rather than the rule. You will be able to develop a strategy specific to your needs.

The following is a summary of the steps you will be following to develop and implement your career plan.

The Artist's Evaluation

At this time, you should have a very good idea of where you have been with your career, where you are now, and where it is you want to be in the next six months, two years, five years, and beyond with your career. You have determined honestly what it is you want to achieve with your career, either financial success or historical importance. Your goals are your own and are very personal. There are no wrong answers in this subject.

The next steps you will take with the aid of this book are the building of your plan and the gathering of the materials and knowledge you will need to successfully execute that plan. Take each step in the building process one at a time until you are comfortable the completion is at hand.

The process of building a career is cyclical throughout your life. At this time, you are stepping possibly for the first time into the process. As you execute your plan and learn more about the world of art, you will make adjustments, research new opportunities, update new materials and so forth. It is a constant evolution of your life as an artist.

Describing Your Art -- Who Are You?

The primary goal in marketing your art is to encourage people to see your art work. Many artists do not make the conscious effort to put into words what their art is about. You will need to describe your art work, the media you use, the style you use, and the philosophy that is the foundation of your work.

In this chapter, you will: Write an Artist's Statement

Marketplaces and Opportunities

Before you begin marketing your art, you should understand what marketplaces are available to you. A well thought-out career and business plan will call for marketing in more than one area; therefore, it is important to realize what options are out there. This will give you a broad knowledge base from which to work as you select your target markets.

In this chapter, you will: Select the primary and secondary marketplaces you wish to pursue in your career plan

Developing Your Presentation Materials

One of the most important steps you take in your career will be to build the presentation materials that will represent you, for without them, you are out of business. Throughout your career, you must continue to develop your work and knowledge. Therefore you will be updating your presentation materials. These materials often will be the only liaison you have between yourself and a potential exhibition or sale.

In this chapter, you will: Assemble your presentation materials

Assemble your archive

Catalog and Brochure -- Design and Development

The catalog is an important part of your presentation. The purpose of the catalog is to elevate your importance as an artist and the importance of your works in the art world. The catalog adds to your credibility, distinguishing you above the masses. Art works and statements seen in print are often taken far more seriously than those that are not.

It is not uncommon for an artist to perceive the need for a catalog but believe that it is out of their financial reach. This is an unfortunate misconception. By following the standard rules for designing an academic catalog and by comparison-shopping the production services you will need, you can develop a professional catalog of your selected works with only a modest investment. But if you still believe that your budget will not let you create a complete catalog at this time, consider a brochure. The brochure will use the same elements as the catalog but in a condensed form, allowing you to produce an effective promotional piece on a smaller scale.

In this chapter, you will: Design and produce an academic catalog of your works

Design and produce an academic brochure of your works

Qualifying Your Targets

You may be a professional artist wishing to expand your exposure to more venues or you may be a part-time artist ready to take a shot at getting your work into a gallery. Either way, this is your chance to show the art world what you are all about, so do not underestimate the importance of doing your "homework." Truly successful artists understand the importance of planning their actions. Aside from your talent and the preparedness of your presentation materials, your knowledge regarding each venue you wish to approach will put you on the right track, saving you time, money, and frustration.

In this chapter, you will:

- Develop a regular teleresearch program
- Develop a record-keeping system for the information you gather
- Maintain a list of viable venues

Presenting Your Work

At this point in your career planning, you will begin to come in contact with people within the art community. Take a moment to tune up your "art etiquette" skills and awareness. These guidelines are applicable whenever you contact people for the purpose of achieving your career goals. Consider and evaluate each facet of "art etiquette" that is posed in this section.

Begin to present your materials to those venues that you have qualified in advance.

In this chapter, you will:

- Evaluate art etiquette questions
- Present your materials to the targeted venues
- Follow up with each presentation
- Develop a record-keeping system to record each contact with the prospective venues, both positive and negative
- Develop your mailing list

Written Communications

The written word can provide great strength to your presentation. It is important for you to be aware of how to write a professional letter properly. There are a number of good books written on the subject that provide the grammatical and structural guidelines appropriate for such communication.

In this chapter, you will:

- Purchase your professional stationery
- Develop your letter library:
  - Cover Letters
  - Follow up Letters
  - Thank-you Notes
- Develop your professional resume

Working with the Venues -- Business and Legal Considerations

As an artist, you will have to undertake the responsibility of signing contracts and agreements pertaining to your work. It is wise for you to have some idea of what is expected of you.

In this chapter, you will:

- Develop your legal document library

Promotions

Your goal with all promotions is to arouse the interest of the art world in your work, to move them to action to see and experience your work and to talk to others about it, further spreading the word. You will employ a variety of means to create this excitement, ranging from printed materials, printed and electronic media, special events, to personal networking. Many of your options are not expensive but simply require ingenuity and perseverance on your part.

In this chapter, you will:

- Prepare for the promotional process
- Develop promotions for your scheduled events
- Develop long-term promotions for your overall career
- Develop a promotions record-keeping process to stay attuned to what "word" is out when

Publishing Your Work

Publishing is often misunderstood. Let us refer to publishing as producing a quantity of work based on the multiplication of a piece. This is referred to as producing "limited editions" or a "series" of pieces. Publishing is not limited to just the painter or photographer. Sculptors and other artisans can also publish their work by creating a piece in bronze, for example, and then casting additional pieces based upon this first piece. The sculptor would then have a limited edition of pieces to display and sell instead of only the single piece.

In this chapter, you will:

- Evaluate the appropriateness of publishing within your career plan
- Develop a publishing plan
- Teleresearch viable publishing companies or your option to self publish
- Establish a method of distribution
- Design and then produce marketing materials for your published works
- Publish your work

Pricing Your Work

Pricing your works is an important aspect of your career plan. It requires a thorough research of the marketplaces you are targeting and the artists who are already selling there. Remember to compare apples to apples and oranges to oranges. Look at the successes of the artists who are similar in style, medium, and importance to yourself. There is no sense in blowing your perceptions out of proportion by following a blue chip artist's sales record, unless that is where you are or where you intend to be. For now, research artists who are similar to yourself.

In this chapter, you will:

- Research the current market prices for artists of similar style, quality and technique
- Develop a wholesale/retail pricing structure for your present body of work

Finding Funding for Your Work

There are many opportunities for an artist to obtain funding for their works through grants, artist-in-residence programs, lecturing at local colleges, schools, universities or artist groups, and sponsorships. With an organized research effort, you may uncover opportunities for aid in which your work fits nicely.

In this chapter, you will: Research funding resources (grants, residency programs, lecturing, benefactors, etc.)

Words from Someone Who Has Been There

If you are an artist who has never tried to obtain representation, remember that you have nothing to lose and everything to gain. It is easy to achieve if you follow a realistic career plan. As you complete this book, you will begin to gain the confidence in yourself, your work, and your approach. Stick with it.

I often ask artists why they have not attempted to show their work. Many times they say they are not ready; but five years later they are still not ready. Sometimes I get the impression that fear of rejection is holding them back. No matter how prepared you are and how good your art work is you are going to get rejections; there is nothing you can do to avoid it. Why some art "makes it" can't be explained in black and white terms. It is a very subjective evaluation so don't hold back. It is only by getting exhibitions under your belt that you will be able to build your confidence, build a biography, accept rejection, and move on.

DESCRIBING YOUR ART -- WHO ARE YOU?

The primary goal in marketing your art is to encourage people to see your art work. If you present your work professionally, people will perceive it that way. When you present yourself clearly and with interest, those to whom you are showing your work will want to believe that your art is interesting.

A rule of thumb to keep in mind is that first impressions occur within the first five seconds of one person meeting another; 70% of that impression is nonverbal (appearance, attitude, body language) and the other 30% is verbal (what you have to say). Now if you apply this rule to your marketing efforts, you can see how the presentation of your materials will weigh heavily in someone's impression of you. Sloppy materials will give a poor impression, and the viewer will probably perceive the art as equally poor. A presentation prepared such as we describe in this book will give a strong and interesting first impression and make the person want to see more. Remember, a big part of the marketing game is first impressions, and first impressions are very hard to change.

Describing Your Art and Yourself

Many artists do not make the conscious effort to put into words what their art is about. It is easier for them to say that they can't describe their work and simply to push slides or pictures at the person they are showing their work to. That won't cut it if you want to successfully market yourself. You would be severely limiting your chance to communicate. You must be able to verbally describe your art work, the media you use, the style you use, and the underlying philosophy of your work. Remember, you have to give of yourself before anyone will give back to you.

The key points to keep in mind when describing your works are: (1) the type of artist you are, (2) the style you work in, (3) the content of your art as described by your philosophy, and (4) your use of the media. Your goal is to give the viewer an idea of what is unique about your work, to pique their interest. Keep your description simple, brief, and honest, whether you are speaking to someone or using the description in printed material.

When writing an "Artist's Statement," keep it to one or two paragraphs and no more than 100 words. Beyond that you are running at the mouth. Stay away from vague, flowery words that have no real descriptive meaning; words that are in "fashion" rather than fact. For example, "opulent but subtle texture" really sounds good, but what does it mean?

If you do not feel secure in what you are writing, take the time to do some research. Read a number of descriptions that have been written about other "successful" artists. You may wish to visit a few galleries and museums to read what has been written in the artists' exhibition catalogs.

You may elect to have another person help write your artist's statement with you. Select someone who is knowledgeable about your style of art. You need not go after the big name art critic, but select a writer who will be positive about your work. ***You can do this yourself if you simply apply the same amount of dedication to this task as you would to one of your art pieces.***

Consistency

One of the biggest challenges you will face in marketing your art is making sure the pieces you choose to present are up to date, consistent with one another, and convey your style and talent. Do not work under the assumption that by showing a variety of styles you are somehow demonstrating the scope of your skills. Such a "pot-luck" portfolio will only damage your potential for representation as few gallery directors are interested in trying to guess which of those styles is "yours." Unless your current work has some strong ties with earlier groupings, avoid showing the two together. ***If you want to be taken seriously, you must produce a body of works whose strength and continuity shows a well-defined sense of direction.***

A prime example of this rule involves an artist I met while working at the museum. He had just returned from presenting his work in New York and was particularly discouraged by the response from one of the more prestigious galleries. The director, a famous and respected figure in the art community, had recommended that the artist "go home to California and take up a new profession." After looking at the work the artist had chosen to present, I could see the director's point. The portfolio contained what the artist felt was a good representation of his art, which might have worked for him had he been organizing a retrospective of everything he'd done since grammar school. Confronted with thirty years of the artist's best works demonstrating a major lack of consistency, the director had every reason to be confused.

Almost as common as lack of continuity is the overabundance of it. If the art you are producing today bears an uncanny resemblance to work you were showing ten or twenty years ago, perhaps it is time for some adaptation. Several years ago, I asked a major collector about her most recent purchases. How did she select the works she was purchasing? "We buy what's happening now," was her response.

If you plan to be included in the sphere of marketable art, it is important to keep abreast of current trends in the art world. I am not suggesting that you change your style with every passing fad, nor would I recommend you copy the styles of the already established "blue chip" artists; their work falls into the category of "what's happening forever." You can, however, expand your work without resorting to major surgery. Fine art and graphic art publications such as ***ArtNews***, ***Art in America*** and others can keep you informed on the current interests of the major galleries and institutions. From there it is simply a matter of experimenting and further developing your work. ***Remember; have conviction in your work and others will too.***

Constructive Criticism

In choosing this profession, you leave yourself open for possible abuse by "would-be" pseudo-critics. So have thick skin, persevere, and always remember, as long as they spell your name correctly, you are in good shape. What is important to understand is that all artists have had "slammings" by critics throughout their careers. It comes with the territory. Always keep in mind that, "an opinion is only an opinion, but a work of art is a fact," however good or bad it may be. ***Only show your best work.***

In 1987, I received a slamming as a museum director. Our museum organized Rufino Tamayo's first major retrospective exhibition on the West Coast. It was a smashing success, and close to 2,000 people attended the opening. Tamayo told me it was the best opening of his work he had ever attended. Numerous art scholars compared the show to his Guggenheim Retrospective of 1979. One local art critic raved about the show and what an opportunity it was for so many people to be in the company of such an important artist on opening night. Another local critic, however, bombed the show as well as Tamayo, claiming he was a "nobody who could only paint stick figures from south of the border."

Seeking out constructive criticism is an important part of your artistic development. Solicit responses about your work from people you respect, not just from those who will tell you how wonderful your art is. Choose people who will be truthful and are knowledgeable enough to evaluate the works. You may find a fellow artist, instructor, curator, or consultant who will set aside time for you if you ask. Remember that they are helping you, so be gracious, keep an open mind and listen. It is not the time to argue your philosophy or style but a time to listen to what another person receives from your work. Think about what the person is telling you, and later, you may either disregard that view or utilize it for your own growth.

I do not recommend changing who you are as an artist every time someone comments on your work. One artist friend was so influenced by artistic reviews in the newspaper that he would change his style on a weekly basis. He changed so often that he never gave himself the opportunity to be recognized for his own good work. As a result, he was never able to fully develop his own style, which was on the verge of becoming very powerful. If you have something that works for you, it is important to have conviction in that work. Know what your work is all about and what gives you inspiration.

MARKETPLACES AND OPPORTUNITIES

No matter what your ambitions for your work, be they modest or extravagant, you will achieve your desired results most readily through step-by-step planning. Before you begin marketing your art, you should understand what marketplaces are available to you. A well-thought-out business and career plan will call for marketing in more than one area; therefore, it is important to realize what options and possibilities are out there for you. This will give you a broad knowledge base from which to work as you select your target markets.

Every venue will have its advantages and disadvantages based on the goals you have set for yourself. A career is a step-by-step progression of attaining goals. One venue may be perfect for giving you the experience and artistic maturity to lead you to another, more prominent venue. Consider all the available options.

There will be venues for which your art is not appropriate. Galleries, museums, and collectors will have their own set of goals and specific focus that they pursue. In the process of qualifying your contacts, you will learn about their focus, which will save you time, money, and frustration.

All venues can be broken down into one of four categories: local, regional, national, and international. Depending upon your prior exposure and success, I suggest you pursue your target markets in that order. Use one level of exhibition to build to the next, then the next and so on. If, for example, you were to try to jump immediately into the international market with a biography of limited exposure, the odds would be against you. With increased exposure comes increased network contacts and support, which is reflected in increased success. ***Take it step by step***. Always look for opportunities to show your work.

One artist I worked with recently obtained gallery representation as a result of always being prepared. While on vacation in the Caribbean, he brought along a presentation package of his work, "just in case." In the course of sight-seeing, the opportunity arose for him to show his work to a dealer in St. Thomas, and after a few brief conversations and a presentation, the dealer offered to represent his work.

Such opportunities for meeting contacts are not limited to artists. One art writer with whom I work, struck up a conversation in a Los Angeles hair salon with the woman who was sitting next to her. As it turned out, the woman was a producer looking for a few new projects. By the end of the conversation, the writer had presented her book to the producer who was not only interested in distributing the book but producing a documentary based on the writer's work. Opportunities can be found almost anywhere.

Fine Art Galleries

A fine art gallery is a place of business in which the primary purpose is to sell art for a profit. This type of gallery is usually more interested in the career and the importance of the artist than are other types of galleries. The fine art gallery generally works on a percentage or consignment basis with the artist. A gallery rarely purchases the artist's works, although this is not unheard of once an artist reaches a certain stature.

Most galleries will have a specific type of art on which they focus. One gallery may sell southwestern art, another watercolors and another contemporary abstracts. A gallery may even limit itself to a specific price range or subject matter. Different levels of fine art galleries exist, ranging from promoters of blue chip artists to the representation of lesser-known artists. It will be your job to qualify the galleries you would like to represent you on the basis of the style of art, price range, and subject matter they sell.

Even among galleries that sell the same type of art, there are varying levels of stature or prominence within the art community. One gallery may be a commercial art supply store with a small exhibition space in the back, whereas another may be a serious, heavily promoted gallery with a very dedicated dealer running the show. Again, you will learn all about the gallery during the qualification process.

There are advantages to exhibiting your art in a gallery. Your work will receive exposure to a larger number of people than it would hanging in your studio. The level of serious exposure will rise with the increased prominence of the gallery. Your art will also receive increased credibility and value by virtue of the notoriety of the other artists showing in the gallery with you. If the gallery represents blue chip artists, your work will be perceived to be of greater importance in the art world.

There are many advantages to being represented by a gallery. Galleries can have large networks within the art community with which to sell and promote the works of their artists. You will be availed to that network by being in their gallery because their goal is to increase the importance of your work and thereby increase their sales. The gallery will hold openings, receptions, and other events dedicated to drawing in more patrons. When a buyer is found for a piece of your work, the dealer or their staff will take care of it. You won't have to deal with haggling over price or value; you will simply receive your percentage of the sale.

There are disadvantages to this situation as well. Because the sales process is taken out of your hands, you will often not meet your collectors personally. This problem can be remedied by efforts on your part to have contact with each person who has purchased your work. A thank-you note or a personal note of appreciation always impresses a collector, and it may open further opportunities; many collectors like to meet the artists. Occasionally, galleries will sell works without providing any records to you. Be sure to include a clause in your agreement stipulating that you are to be provided records of the collectors of your work should the gallery go out of business.

Some galleries may not be as aggressive as others in promoting your work through events and printed materials. Promotion of your work may be a shared responsibility between you and the gallery. If there is a time or financial constraint hindering the gallery from showing your work, jump in and offer to help, if necessary. Your goal is to break down any barriers -- within reason -- that are stopping the gallery from showing your works. The benefit of your involvement will be both yours and the gallery's. When you are starting out, you may consider offering to share in the cost of invitations or to help in the organization of press releases, etc. This may open the door by making you more attractive than another artist to the gallery. Confirm all arrangements for reimbursement of expenses in writing prior to beginning the work. Remember, do not let walls be put up over small issues. Get the exhibition; that is what will help you move on in your career.

I do believe that in the beginning of an artist's career, he or she may have to make compromises as with any other business. The main thing you must keep in mind is that without shows, your opportunity for sales, recognition, and the building of your career will not happen.

Commercial Galleries

A commercial gallery, like its fine art counterpart, is a place of business in which the sole purpose is to sell art for a profit. However, unlike the fine art gallery, the commercial gallery is focused on selling a "product" and not necessarily on promoting the career of the artist. The works that are displayed in a commercial gallery are usually consumer oriented. Most commercial galleries deal in originals; however, you might see an artist's "product line" of framed prints, unframed prints, greeting cards, t-shirts, and so forth for sale in this type of gallery. Different levels of commercial galleries range from frame shops and boutiques, which often show lesser-known artists, to sophisticated galleries that show works by blue chip artists.

The staff of commercial galleries are salespeople. It is their goal to sell anything and everything that is hanging on their walls. They often know very little about art or even about the artist who created the works they are selling. They are not art dealers with networks of serious collectors or institutional contacts. The salespeople are only interested in one thing: selling!

If you are concerned primarily with making sales, this is the type of gallery you might consider. A commercial gallery can generate revenues on a regular basis. A number of artists I work with deal entirely with this type of gallery, and many do very well. One of these artists has a gallery in his home town that features his work. He averages $8,000 per month in sales and has developed a product line focused on the tourist trade in that community. His work is priced at a level that is easy for the average consumer to afford.

The advantage of showing in this type of gallery is the increased exposure to the general public for the purpose of making sales. The art pieces revolve in and out of the gallery within a reasonable amount of time, or the consigned pieces are simply returned to you unsold. While your work is popular and selling well, you will have a very dedicated venue. But never forget to continue to work on and expand your product line, as at some point your work may become less popular. Never become complacent with your current marketplace or product.

There are disadvantages to commercial galleries for the fine artist who wishes to promote the importance of his or her work beyond the individual sale. The commercial gallery will not work to support your career with the same dedication as does the fine art gallery. Blue chip collectors, museums, and universities who can heavily influence your career do not buy or show works from this type of gallery. Carefully choose your direction and those who represent you.

Even if you are a commercial artist primarily concerned with sales, reliance on a single gallery of this type will limit the possibilities. At first you may be the primary focus of the gallery. But your work can just as easily be put at the back of the gallery when ownership changes hands or the focus of the gallery changes. Keep in tune with what is happening at the galleries.

Gallery Chains

The gallery chain is usually a commercial gallery with many exhibition spaces or "stores" in different geographical locations that work in cooperation with one another. These galleries deal with a broad spectrum of artists, from the very famous to the lesser-known. The established artist gives stability to the gallery's stable of artists and keeps the gallery's credibility high.

The gallery chains have a more commercial approach than do the traditional galleries. The chain handles quality prints of famous artists and heavily advertises and promotes them. Then, hung alongside a print by a famous or recognized artist may be an original of a lesser-known artist. When the viewing public comes into the gallery, the lesser-known artist's original painting is perceived as of similar value as the quality print of the famous artist. This is a common marketing tactic used by the gallery to present a relatively unknown artist to a less experienced collector, representing it as a good value in comparison. Thus the gallery takes advantage of the best of both worlds, using the notoriety of the established artist to promote the value of the lesser known artist.

A gallery chain can be good for an artist for a number of reasons. Because the work receives exposure in a number of geographic locations, the opportunity for a higher volume of sales exists because of sheer numbers.

The decision to handle an artist's work usually comes from a main office, not from a single gallery location. Make sure you are ready to produce enough works, whether originals or prints, to make it worth the gallery's time. A number of artists I have worked with would not be able to work with gallery chains because they cannot produce enough work to supply the galleries. This is where developing a publishing plan, as we discuss in the chapter "Publishing Your Work," to increase the production of art so you can satisfy the gallery's needs. Keep your options open.

Artist Co-Op Galleries

A "co-op" or cooperative gallery is where a group of artists have joined together to rent exhibition space in which to show their art. The artists share all costs equally including the costs of promoting and holding shows, openings, receptions, etc. In turn, the profits from the sales of art through this space are also shared. The division of sales receipts is agreed upon among the artists. If you have not shown much or are having a hard time obtaining representation, this type of space is a good option.

Co-op galleries can be a good way to show your works hung in a gallery setting. These types of galleries are also a good way to learn firsthand about promotions and sales. The next time you approach a gallery to show your works, you will have a better understanding of what the gallery must consider.

In selecting a co-op gallery, remember location is extremely important as well as the artists who are showing there. Check them out by attending some of their shows and talking to other artists.

Art Dealers

An art dealer is a person who deals in the sale of art. There are different types of art dealers, often they are the owner or director of a gallery. Most dealers will have specific types of art on which they focus.

A gallery dealer can be an important influence on your career. The art business is a lot like any business; it's who you know. For instance, if you are an artist seeking to have exposure in museums, it is important for you to attain representation by a dealer who is somehow connected to these types of institutions. This will vastly improve your chances of obtaining museum exhibitions. Ask the dealer whether they know someone in the museum world who could help you. Keep on your toes and be alert to the opportunities that present themselves to you.

A very important fact to keep in mind is that a good art dealer will have collectors who can add to the importance of your work. If your work is purchased by one of their important collectors, your work will most likely be elevated in importance. Remember, it is the company your art keeps that can enhance the importance of your work. As other collectors hear of the purchase by one of their peers, the more apt they are to become interested in collecting your work. Now your work will be in the company of other important artists' works.

By all means, do not be a snob about obtaining a dealer, but always be thorough in your qualification of representation. You need to open avenues for exposure of your art, but most preferably with a dealer who has earned a good reputation for his or her work. One of my artist friends had an unfortunate experience with a Dallas gallery. My friend shipped a number of his sculpture pieces to this gallery with a written commitment to exhibit the work over a one-month period. The agreement allowed the artist to recoup the costs of shipping with the first sale. When inquiries were made to confirm receipt of the marble pieces, no one at the gallery seemed to know anything. Finally, the dealer said all the pieces were damaged in shipping and were useless for the show; should they be thrown out? This so alarmed the artist that he jumped in a rented truck and drove to Dallas. When he arrived, he found the crates had not even been opened. No damage had occurred. The gallery itself had simply gone out of business and could not live up to its commitments.

The moral of this story is to find the very best dealer you can to represent your work. Be selective about whom you choose. Find out whom they already represent, whom their collectors are, and so forth. As you qualify your targeted galleries, you will also qualify their dealers.

Independent Dealers

An independent dealer is also an individual who handles the sale of art. He or she often does not have a gallery or exhibition space. The independent dealer may be a former curator, gallery dealer, or art-related professional who works directly from his or her home or office. As with the gallery dealer, the independent may often focus on a specific type of art although some will sell and broker a wide variety of art.

Independent dealers may locate space for an exhibition in rental spaces, restaurants, building lobbies, or other galleries. When working in collaboration with a gallery, independent dealers will bring their stable of artists to the gallery for exhibition. Some of these dealers will use their home as a gallery.

An independent dealer may have great networking channels that they have developed, as well as access to collectors, museums, institutions, and other opportunities. Again, be selective about whom you choose to represent you. Find out whom they already represent, who their collectors are, and so forth. Qualify the independent dealer as thoroughly as you would the gallery dealer.

Corporate Art Consultants (Dealers)

The corporate art consultant is an art dealer who sells art to companies and institutions (hotels, hospitals, accountancy firms, law firms, architectural firms, property management companies, etc.). This type of dealer operates much as the gallery dealer does, often times having a small gallery space.

The consultant often works with companies who are either in an expansion phase, revamping their image, or redecorating their offices. Occasionally, consultants will have a corporate client who owns an important collection for which they act as curator, developing and selecting works for the collection. These dealers have many projects going on at one time, which means more opportunities for your work to sell. Many consultants work with decorators, designers, municipalities, and so on, networking in these areas to keep on top of what businesses are in an expansion or redevelopment mode.

This is the type of dealer that best represents muralists, portrait painters, and commission artists. Unlike a gallery exhibiting a solo show once or twice a year, consultants are filling the requests of their clientele on a daily basis. This can be of major financial benefit to the artists and can keep them very busy.

Sales from Your Studio -- CAUTION!

Direct sales from your studio can be a great way to make sales, but remember to take advantage of other opportunities available to you as well. Many collectors like to meet and deal directly with the artist. If you are not represented by a gallery and you are willing to do the leg work, I recommend studio sales. It allows people to get to know you and your work and may open other opportunities. You may consider having a studio show once or twice a year. The best times are November to early December and early summer, but not too close to April 15th.

A word of CAUTION. You must handle your studio sales diplomatically, or you may lose the gallery representation you worked very hard to attain. If you are represented by a gallery in close proximity to your studio, you run the high risk of losing them by competing with rather than supporting their sales efforts. Most galleries frown on artists who sell out of the "back door" of their studios. Once you have a reputation for doing this, galleries will not touch you. Word travels fast in the art world.

One artist in my local community always appeared to sell his work well in our area, although it was never through gallery representation. I was curious as to why he was never able to attain a gallery. I found the opportunity to ask this question at a local opening and found out to my surprise that he had been black-balled by the local dealers for selling his work at a greatly discounted price directly from his studio. He had gained the reputation for circumventing his gallery to make direct sales to people who saw his work in the gallery. The dealer was less than pleased and dealt with it directly.

Artists who are represented by galleries outside their vicinity can successfully sell directly from their studios with the knowledge of their dealer. It is important to maintain price integrity with your gallery to not undercut their efforts. Again, if you sabotage the work they have done to increase the value of your art, you run the high risk of losing your representation.

If you do decide to sell from your studio, you may consider giving your gallery 5% to 10% of your sales. This will show that your loyalties remain with them. A dealer would feel comfortable sending a client to meet you, knowing that you are honestly working in collaboration with his or her efforts.

Museums

Museums are institutions for which the primary purpose is to exhibit works of art and provide cultural enrichment to their community. They are not there to sell your work, although posters or limited editions may be available to the general public through the gift shop. A piece on loan from a gallery to a museum may be sold during an exhibition but not removed until after the exhibit is over. In this case, it is not unusual for the museum to receive a percentage of the sale out of courtesy from the dealer, but again, the museum is not there to sell works of art.

The importance of the first impression you make as a professional artist could never be more important than when presenting your work to a museum. The key to attaining a museum curator's attention is to present a well-organized package and a strong body of work. The type of presentation package used for a museum should be academic and ***not*** commercial. (This book will show you how to develop an academic presentation in later chapters.)

Every museum will have specific types of art on which they focus. One museum may exhibit regional art of varying styles, whereas another exhibits contemporary art from Europe, and so on. A museum may limit itself to a specific subject matter, such as western art. It will be your job to qualify your target museum on the basis of the work they exhibit.

Even among museums of similar focus, there are varying levels of stature or prominence. One museum may be a local community endeavor whose patronage is primarily the community in which it is located; another may be a nationally known organization with high visibility. Again, you should qualify your museum for its prominence in the art community before contacting them about your work.

There are many advantages to exhibiting your work in a museum. The primary reason for exhibiting your work in a museum is to enhance your exposure in an academic setting. A museum exhibition will increase the credibility of your work, demonstrating to the art world that your work has institutional acceptance and is important. Do not discount group shows in blind pursuit of that "one-man" show. Group shows with known artists can work to enhance the importance of your art within the art world.

Museums, as do galleries, hold openings and receptions that serve to promote the exhibition. These events are generally well attended by virtue of the fact that they are held by a museum. You receive exposure to an art-viewing public who will be more educated about what they are viewing. Whenever an event is held in conjunction with your show, you ***must*** attend. It is of great importance to your career to attend all such events. Remember, the people you "snub" on the way up the ladder of success may one day be met as you come down that ladder.

The museum curators and directors can be important and often influential people in the art world. As with the art dealers, the curators can have a tremendous influence on your career. If they are supportive of your work, they will feel comfortable in promoting you to other institutions as well as to their own museum for future shows. The curators can present your work to their serious patrons and connect you with their network of contacts.

Museums often have funds for acquisitions. The director, curator, and in some cases, an acquisition committee will select the works to be purchased for the collection. Keep in mind when selling to a museum that they may expect to receive a reduction in price. You may wish to offer a reduced price before you are asked. It is considered an honor for an institution to purchase one of your pieces for their collection, as this can be a boost to your career. Consider donating your work to a museum. Each institution will have its own policy regarding what can be accepted as donations and may not accept your work initially. If one does, it is truly a boost to your career.

There are a few "inconveniences" to exhibiting in a museum. Do not expect sales to occur as you would with a gallery. When your art is in a museum exhibition, it will not be available for any other venue until the show is over.

Museums are perceived as difficult to get into, especially if you are not ready. You should realize that a museum is an academic institution, and therefore your work must be presented in an academic manner. A museum will not be interested in commercial artwork, and if your presentation is too slick and commercial in nature, your work will be perceived in that way. Follow the presentation instructions provided in later chapters to guide you.

Museum Sales and Rental Galleries

Although a museum's primary focus is the exhibition of art to their community, many museums will have sales and rental galleries to sell or rent an artist's works to individuals or corporations. The museum usually works on a percentage basis with their selected artists.

In making art available for rent, the museum provides the patron an opportunity either to enjoy a piece without the large initial investment or to take the piece on a trial basis before purchasing. This can provide the artist with a nominal continuous income. Museums, on an average, will sell 30% of all rental art. The renting patron often becomes "attached" to a piece and may in turn purchase it. I recommend pursuing this option if it is geographically feasible for you.

In targeting museums, you should ask about the policies regarding their rental gallery. First, check it out, and make sure your art fits the focus of the museum's gallery. You may inquire about acquisitions made by the museum: whom to contact, and how artists submit their work for possible sales from their collection.

Traveling Museum Exhibitions

A traveling museum exhibition is a highly organized exhibition of art that travels from one museum to the next in different geographical locations. There are a number of companies as well as museums that organize these exhibitions. This allows each organization to share the expense of organizing and promoting the exhibition. All facets of a traveling show are usually well orchestrated, from the selection of the art pieces to the presentation, public relations materials, and catalogs to the changing of the exhibition itself.

The likelihood of a unestablished artist being selected for one of these exhibitions is very slim. However, a traveling show can be very important to one's career. And you simply never know what opportunities may arise. Keep the concept of a traveling exhibition in mind when you are organizing your presentation materials. Your presentation can present your works both individually or as a full exhibition ready and able to be hung immediately.

I was recently asked to help organize an exhibition of twelve artists in a local gallery. The show was designed around a selected focus, and the works all related to each other based on that focus. The artists joined together to share the costs of producing a forty-eight page catalog for the show. Once the show was hung, I presented the exhibition to venues outside our local area using the catalog. As a result, this exhibition was immediately booked into two additional venues. The new venues will also be able to use the catalog and promotional materials the artists prepared for the original event. Galleries and institutions like to show exhibits that are well organized because it reflects positively on their image and requires less work and expense. Always keep this fact in mind.

Curators for Corporate or Private Collections

Corporations and some collectors often hire curators to develop their art collections. The curator of such collections usually has an academic background and a specialized knowledge of the specific art the employer collects. A collector, as does a gallery and a museum, will focus on a given artist, period of art, style, subject matter, or other criteria important to the collector.

The curator's job is to find works that will enhance the collection, increasing its importance. A good curator who handles an important collection can be of great value to your career. If your work is purchased by their collector, it will elevate your importance. Again, remember it is the company your art keeps that will help influence the importance of your work and your career.

If you intend to approach a curator of a corporate or private collection, you must know what type of work he or she collects. A good dealer or museum curator can open the door for you as well as make sure that you are prepared when you solicit these types of collectors.

Publishing

Fine art publishing is the process of creating multiple editions of your work through limited editions, mixed media prints, stone lithography and posters. The goals of publishing are to increase the exposure of your art to the public, open other markets for the sales of your art to those to whom it would otherwise be unavailable, and increase the value of your original works by enhancing the recognition of your art. It is my opinion that if you wish to make a living with your art, publishing is a great way to go if your work is suited for it.

There are many fine art publishers throughout the country. Each would like to discover the next Pablo Picasso, but more than likely they are looking for artists whose work has the potential to sell. Publishers will often focus on particular styles of art - styles with which they have had success in the past and for which their production and distribution resources are attuned. When you are ready to approach a publisher, make sure you know what they have printed in the past. Try to learn what they may be planning to print in the future. It is beneficial to have a track record of sales and desirability for your work, but it's not necessary if your work is right for the publisher. This is where your gallery and museum exhibitions will be of benefit to you. Everyone is looking for an artist with credibility.

Publishing can be especially useful to the artist whose works require a great deal of time to complete. Many artists believe the financial burden of publishing lies solely with the publisher. Some publishers may be more attracted to an artist who is willing to share the financial risk of producing the art works than to an artist who is not, especially if the artist is an unknown with no real track record in publishing. For example, if you are willing to share the costs of producing the prints and to share a percentage of the profits, you may be more attractive than the artist who says "you pay for the printing and distribution and give me everything." Remember, 100% of nothing is nothing.

We will discuss publishing in great detail later on.

Commissions

Commissions are works of art produced specifically for a given collector, individual, corporation, business, or museum. Individuals may pay the artist to create a work specifically for them. In essence, you are being paid to work within given guidelines, whatever they may be.

Commission work can be financially rewarding but I would not recommend relying solely on this type of work for your exclusive income. You can obtain commissions through galleries, art dealers, consultants, and interior designers or by yourself through your own studio or other promotions. If your art lends itself to this type of work, it can be a good way to round out your marketing plan and also provide a steady income once you become established.

Art Fairs and Shows

Art fairs are a good way for artists who produce decorative or more aesthetically pleasing art to sell their work directly to the public. If your work is avant-garde, you probably will not find success through these venues. I know many artists who make a decent living traveling from one fair to the next throughout the year. They often are very prolific artists who also have produced limited editions of their works to be sold. It is a lot of work traveling from place to place, but you can be financially successful by virtue of the sheer numbers of people you will come in contact with.

A number of artists I work with concentrate their efforts on art fairs throughout the country. One artist in particular travels to the fairs almost every weekend. When we discussed what he was able to earn at one of these events, I was quite surprised. He would often generate around $5,000 each weekend with originals and prints of his work. It can be done, especially if your work is reasonably popular and you are willing to work very hard.

These fairs are often sponsored by local or regional art organizations, charities, and clubs. You will find numerous fairs that charge a fee for the privilege to show in their fair as well as take a small percentage of your gross sales. Art fairs are wonderful places to get a reading of how the public responds to your work. Be sure to know ahead of time that your work is the style shown in this particular type of fair.

A number of very prestigious and exclusive art shows are held throughout the year. These shows exhibit much of the very best contemporary fine art as well as what the commercial arts scene has to offer. Such exhibitions are by invitation only and usually require a well-connected dealer to be accepted. It would be worth your while to visit one or more of these shows to see firsthand the art that is making it out there in the "real world."

Juried Shows and Competitions

A juried show is very much like a gallery show, only the pieces being exhibited are reviewed and judged against one another by a panel of critics, curators, art dealers, college professors, art organization directors or any variety of professionals from the community. A juried show may be sponsored by a museum, local university, nonprofit organization, governmental, or civic group.

Such competitions present awards and monetary prizes but the art work is not always required to be "for sale." The purpose of entering a competition is to gain acceptance from the art world rather than to close a sale. Earning a juried award can serve to validate your artistic importance to the art community. Your art may sell by virtue of its exposure during the competition, but sales are not the primary focus.

Winning a juried competition requires a bit of strategy. Select the type of competition that is conducive to the type of art you create. Don't select a juried show for watercolorists if you work in acrylics or oils. I work with one artist who will even make a few phone calls to find out who is on the judging panel of the competition, and then he tailors his piece to the likes of the jury. He greatly enhances his chances of winning an award by doing this kind of homework ahead of time.

There are disadvantages to juried competitions. You have absolutely no input or control over the decisions made about your art. You may have no explanation about what the judges' thinking was in awarding a prize to another artist or yourself. This can be frustrating for the artist, but keep in mind that the visibility of your work is what is most important.

Locating upcoming juried shows in your area is a rather easy task. Keep on top of what is happening in your community by attending college exhibitions, gallery shows, local museums, art supply stores, and the like. Inquire at each of these places as to what competitions may be happening in the future. Subscribe to a number of art magazines; each lists competitions in the back of the publication. Join a local or national arts organization as they often provide such information to their members.

Some competitions charge a fee to process your work. If the fees are reasonable, it may be worth your time and energy to enter. An artist I know asked my opinion about whether she should enter an exhibition in Japan. The entry fee was $300 and the show was accepting only 20 artists from among 300 to 400 entries. I asked her who were some of the artists selected in the past. She read the list, and it was composed of the standard blue chip regulars. My advice to her was to keep the $300, buy more supplies for new works, and look for competitions that are not so likely to be politically influenced. This is not meant to be discouraging, but the art world is very political. If you are not dealing within a given political arena, you may find yourself on the outside looking in.

Schools and Universities

Schools and universities are venues that artists who are not students often disregard. They believe that this type of venue is open only to students, but that's not true. Schools have schedules of shows, exhibitions and competitions throughout the year to which the public may submit their work. These are worthwhile venues to show your work, as they add another academic credential to your biography. These exhibitions will allow your work to be shown not only to students and faculty but also to the public and the media, as art critics often attend such shows. Exhibitions in such academic settings are very good for building your biography.

State and County Fairs

Throughout the country, state and county fairs are held. These fairs showcase a variety of community interests including the arts -- most often the commercial arts. A fair can be a good place to exhibit your works and expand your exposure. Again, it gives you an avenue to learn about the public's reaction to your art. Many large fairs hold juried competitions and give out awards in a variety of categories, while allowing the artists to sell their works at the same time.

One artist I worked with in the past showed his art every year at the Los Angeles County Fair. Well over 150,000 people viewed his art. He received a number of commissions as well as inquiries from galleries as a result.

If you are interested in showing at a fair, contact the appropriate state or county fairgrounds or agricultural commission to obtain their application forms.

Fund-raisers

It is my strong belief that all artists should contribute at least a few of their works to one or two fund-raising events every year. Fund-raisers are socially conscious activities that not only expose your works to the public but also benefit a worthwhile cause.

There are many types of fund-raisers you can approach. In my opinion, museum auctions are the best type for donating your work, as those who attend already have a love for the arts. The lists of philanthropic fund-raisers are endless. Some organizations will ask for a total donation, and some will give a percentage back to the artist. Contact the organization to find out what its policies are.

Select one or two museum auctions to donate your work to each year. Call your local museums and ask them to send you any information they may have regarding their annual auction fund-raiser. You may receive a number of "thank you, but no thank you" responses to the presentation of your works, but don't let that bother you. Simply keep pursuing your goals by presenting your work.

Corporate Loans

Artists, dealers, galleries, and museums may approach large companies and institutions with art works available on loan. The company is given the opportunity to hang quality works of art in their offices without having to purchase. It allows the company to project a successful image without reaching deeply into their pockets. For the artist, it generates a little money and provides a storage space for the work. This is much like the museum sales and rental gallery.

Some organizations will ask you to lend a piece without reimbursement. You may wish to give this some thought, as your art will be exposed daily to the public rather than hidden away. You never know who may see your work at the company offices and, in turn, purchase a piece for themselves. Select strong pieces, but not necessarily those you may wish to put into a gallery or museum exhibition in the near future.

A note of importance: it is imperative that you have a clear, written, and signed agreement regarding your retained ownership of the art and the terms by which the loan will be governed. Include a clause that will allow you to terminate the loan should a buyer or exhibition for the piece be found. You may reserve the right to substitute a piece upon the approval of the other party. Refer to the sample "Loan" document provided in the business and legal considerations chapter.

Religious Organizations

Religious organizations can provide a positive venue for your work. Many organizations have spaces that can be converted easily for exhibitions. Shows held in such spaces become a focused event for the community, drawing attention to your works not only by the congregation but also often by the local media.

I recently was approached to exhibit my works at a Southern California church. My art challenges religious and social beliefs, both positively and negatively. The exhibition created controversy within the church, which served to heighten the exposure of the work; 5,000 people attended the opening event. For me, it was the most interesting exhibition because of the responses from the audience.

Each faith will have its own guidelines for the appropriateness of exhibiting works of art within its halls of worship. Before approaching this venue, it would be wise for you to understand the guidelines and assess your work in this light. It will be important for you to have the support of the organizing committee before finalizing the exhibition arrangements.

Libraries

Libraries are another interesting venue you may wish to pursue. They function to educate the community they serve and often will organize an art show focusing on a certain style, era, or social issue. Art organizations that do not have their own space frequently use libraries for shows. Contact your local libraries for a schedule of exhibitions they are planning. If they do not have any in mind, you may wish to propose a show for them. This again is where using the concept of a traveling show may be to your benefit. You may even wish to lend or donate a piece to the library for display.

Restaurants, Bars, and Other Public Facilities

Artists, dealers, galleries, and museums may approach a variety of public places with art works available for display at little or no cost. A restaurant, for example, is given the opportunity to hang quality works of art without making a large outlay of funds. This allows the restaurant to project a successful image without spending money to purchase the art. For the artist, it can generate money and provide exposure of the works to the public. You can open up opportunities for sales and other exhibitions this way. Everyone involved can win in this situation.

Make sure that when you are showing your work in this type of space you provide the right type of labels and information sheets listing your phone number and address or if you have representation, that of your dealer. If the facility has an opening for you, make sure your works are there on time and you are present for the event. This is a venue where good pre-exhibition promotions are very important.

Interior Designers

Interior designers are always looking for art to use in their projects. They may act as a dealer using your works wherever possible. This will increase the exposure of your work and your sales, as a good designer may have many jobs going at one time.

Interior designers are also good sources for commission works. They are often looking for a work of art that will complete a room. Often, the works designers look for are more commercial, but they do not rule out the more sophisticated fine arts. The work will most likely be selected for its decorative value rather than for its artistic importance.

Trading/Barter

Many artists find that they are able to exchange their works for needed services, including everything from photography, printing, and legal work to computers, jewelry and so on. There is almost no limit to the kinds of things you can trade art for with an interested party. One artist I know trades art each year with a large barter organization for meal coupons at fine restaurants throughout the community. This way, he explains, he is able to dine economically at the same restaurants his collectors frequent.

Focus on the Long-Term Goals of Your Career Plan

Whatever path you choose to pursue in your career, it is important for you to remain consistent in your plan, choosing marketplaces and opportunities which complement each other. Carefully choose your direction and those who represent you. Always keep your goals and plan in mind as you promote, exhibit and sell your work.

As an example, artists who sell their work in commercial galleries will have a difficult time promoting their work to museums. However, artists who sell their work through fine art galleries can more easily transition to the museum venues as the works have not been perceived as "commercial" even though they have been for sale. The artist who sells their work from the back of their studio in a manner which circumvents the efforts of their dealer will quickly lose their representation and in time, find it very difficult to obtain new representation.

Do not allow the temptation to make "the quick buck" overshadow your ultimate goals. If the opportunity does not fit into your overall career plan, it is best to turn it down. Otherwise, you will become your career's own worst enemy, having created inconsistencies in the identity of you and your art. There is nothing wrong with choosing to be a commercial artist, simply remember that once you have made that choice it will be difficult to then take your work back into the fine art arena. Develop your plan based upon your long-term goals, then pursue that plan in all your efforts.

CAREER PLAN

Market Selection Worksheet

This worksheet lists all the potential markets discussed in this chapter. The applicability of each venue for the fine arts versus the commercial arts is noted to the right. Place a check mark in the box next to each venue you wish to include at some point in your career plan. You may not feel ready to approach the venue immediately but would like to at some point in your career.

Rank the priority of each selected venue within your career goals by: 1-highest priority, 2-moderate priority, 3-low priority, and 4-would be nice if it fits in. This will establish the order in which you will address the venue as you begin working your plan.

Market	Order of Priority	Fine Art Venue	Commercial Art Venue
✓ Fine Arts Gallery	1	X	
__ Commercial Gallery	______	X	X
__ Gallery Chain	______	X	X
__ Co-op Gallery	______	X	X
✓ Art Dealer	1	X	X
✓ Independent Art Dealer	2	X	X
✓ Corporate Art Consultant	3	X	X
✓ Studio Sales (Caution!)	1	X	X
✓ Museums	1	X	
✓ Museum Sales/Rental Gallery	2	X	
__ Traveling Museum Shows	______	X	
✓ Curator for Collections	1	X	
✓ Publishing	2	X	X
__ Commissions	______	X	X
__ Art Fairs & Shows	______	X	X
__ Juried Shows & Competitions	______	X	X
✓ Schools & Universities	2	X	X
__ State & County Fairs	______	X	X
✓ Fund-raisers	1	X	X
__ Corporate Loans	______	X	X
✓ Religious Groups	4	X	X
__ Libraries	______	X	X
__ Restaurants, Bars, etc.	______	X	X
__ Interior Designers	______	X	X
__ Trade/Barter	______	X	X

DEVELOPING YOUR PRESENTATION MATERIALS

The single most important section of this book is this chapter, for without your presentation materials, you are out of business. Throughout your career you must continue to develop your work and knowledge. Therefore, you will be continually updating your presentation materials. These materials will often be the only liaison you will have between yourself and a potential exhibition or sale.

The presentation package will be speaking for you. Remember, first impressions occur within the first five seconds of one person meeting another (or one's art), and at least 70% of that first impression relies on the nonverbal factors of your presentation. This chapter and the next (referring to catalogs) will show you how to make sure your materials will live up to their responsibility.

Commercial versus Academic

The presentation of commercial art differs greatly from that of fine art. Materials used for an academic fine art presentation can also be used for a commercial presentation, but the reverse is not true. Commercial presentation materials are not acceptable for use in an academic venue.

Commercial materials are designed to sell the ***artist*** and to generate revenue. Academic materials promote the importance of the ***art*** - the historical comparison of the art to other important works, and the significance of the artist's progression in development to the art world.

Commercial materials are usually "slick" sales tools. Strong adjectives are used heavily within the text of a commercial piece, as shown in the first example on the next page. In contrast, an academic statement would emphasize the art rather than the artist, as shown in the second sample.

These examples show the same artist presented in two completely different ways. The presentation materials described in this book are based on the more academic approach. They can serve you well in both the academic and the commercial venue.

Don't Let Your Presentation Materials Outshine Your Work

This statement is simple but quite true. The art works that are represented by your materials must be your strongest pieces. An evaluation of your present body of works by a consultant, other art professional or through our Artist Evaluation Service is a wise investment at this time. You may even find that you will need to go back to the studio to create a number of stronger pieces to round out your presentation. Make that decision before you begin developing your presentation materials.

Esoteric Statement

I try to delve into the inner thoughts of my imagination, always reflecting upon the inner quadrants of my soul to transform reality, searching the innermost recesses of my life. My intensity and commitment to spiritual growth allows my work to be a beacon focused on transformation.

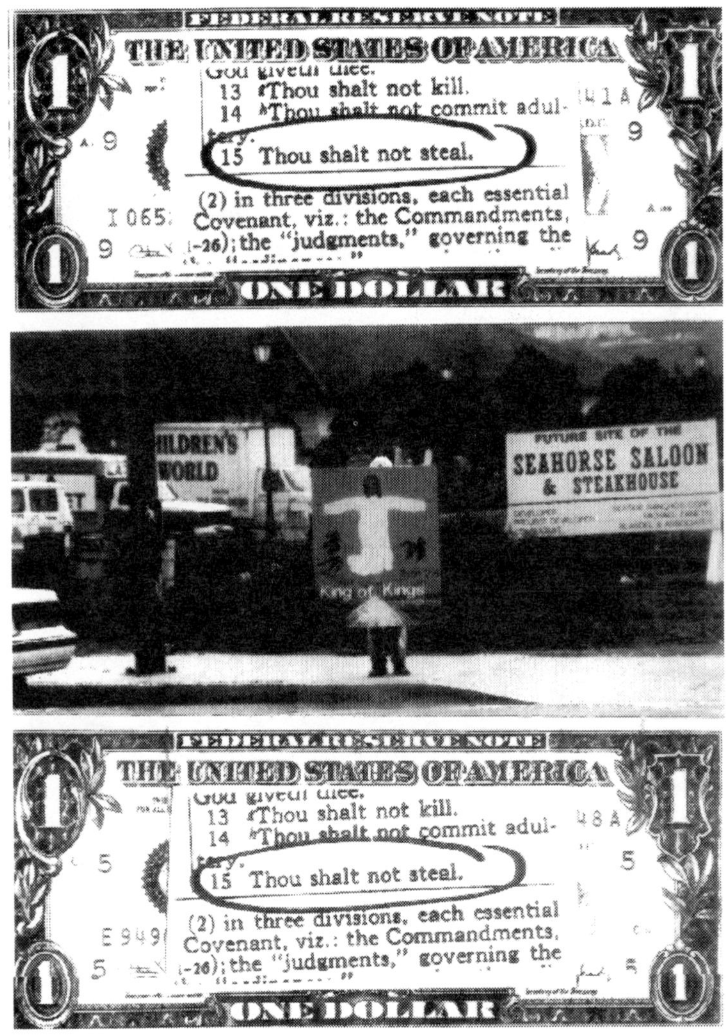

Academic Statement

My paintings are inspired by the people and things around me. I reproduce my paintings from photographs I take of people I meet in places. My art is an accurate reflection of the time in which we live.

The Total Package

You will be developing two specific presentation packages; one is a portion of the other. The first complete package will be your master, serving as the foundation of your archive. The archive consists of all presentation materials, resumes, promotional materials, invitations, newspaper and magazine reviews, referral letters, slides, and photographs pertaining to your work. This archive will be the chronological record of your development as an artist throughout your career.

A portion of this archive will be the academic presentation materials you will use to build your career. When you are soliciting a gallery or museum, for example, you will present only those materials that are pertinent to their needs. In time, if there is to be a retrospective of your work, they may want delve into the entirety of your archive.

You will learn how to use your materials properly to give the most professional presentation possible. Keep in mind that the formats provided here are by no means the only correct methods but are those with which I have repeatedly obtained the desired results. As you expose yourself to the art community, you may come across a new idea that will work for you, so don't be afraid to incorporate that idea into your presentation. However, remember that these materials are to be academic in style and content, not commercial.

Presentation Checklist

Presentation Materials: (see the visual images provided on the following pages)

1. Cover letter

2. Catalog, brochure, or biography page

3. Three (3) 8" x 10" or 8-1/2" x 11" color photographs

4. Two (2) 8" x 10" or 8-1/2" x 11" black and white photographs

5. Properly labeled slides of all pieces shown in the catalog or brochure

6. Sample press releases and promotional materials ready for print (optional)

7. Self-addressed stamped envelope for return of the package/padded envelope for initial presentation of the package

Remaining Archive Materials:

8. An up-to-date academic resume (updated throughout your career)

9. Letters received from dealers, curators, etc. discussing your works (positive or negative)

10. Black & white installation photographs

11. Photographs of important people attending your show

12. Invitations to shows/exhibitions

13. Press releases regarding shows/exhibitions

14. All promotional materials for each show/exhibition

15. Newspaper reviews of your works/shows/exhibitions (positive or negative)

16. Magazine reviews of your works/shows/exhibitions

17. Brochures, tear sheets, etc.

18. Any and all remaining materials referencing you or your works within the context of the art community

Presentation Checklist
Summary Review

Cover Letter

The presentation cover letter is designed to introduce you and your art to the prospective venue.

Catalog, Brochure, or Biography Page

The purpose of the catalog is to elevate your importance as an artist and the importance of your work in the art world. It can range from a condensed four-page brochure to a full nine-, twelve- or twenty-image catalog. If your current finances do not allow for either a catalog or brochure, use a biography sheet. As soon as you are able, replace it with the brochure or catalog. You should use at least one of these printed materials in your presentation.

Photographic Prints (color and black & white)

The color prints support the printed materials, showing the detail of a few select pieces. The black-and-white prints show the recipient that you are aware and ready for promotion of your work.

Color Slides (9, 12, or 20 images)

The color slides support each image printed in your catalog or brochure. Use slide sheets that match the number of images in your printed materials: for example, a nine-slide sheet for a nine-image presentation. Never present a package where empty spaces exist in the slide sheet.

Padded mailing envelope and self-addressed, stamped return envelope

The padded mailing envelope supported with cardboard sheets will properly protect your presentation package. The self-addressed, stamped return envelope is enclosed to help ensure that you will receive your package back after it has been reviewed. The cardboard sheets will be reused to provide support to the return package.

Press Packet (optional)

A press packet is optional in your presentation. It serves to show that your work has been actively exhibited in the community. The prospective venue will see what type of responses you have received in prior exhibitions, again making the prospect of exhibiting your work even more attractive. For example, a museum invitation is especially attractive to a gallery and gives you a great deal of credibility. A positive article from a newspaper or magazine can be copied and included if you feel it will help.

COMPLETE PRESENTATION MATERIALS

1

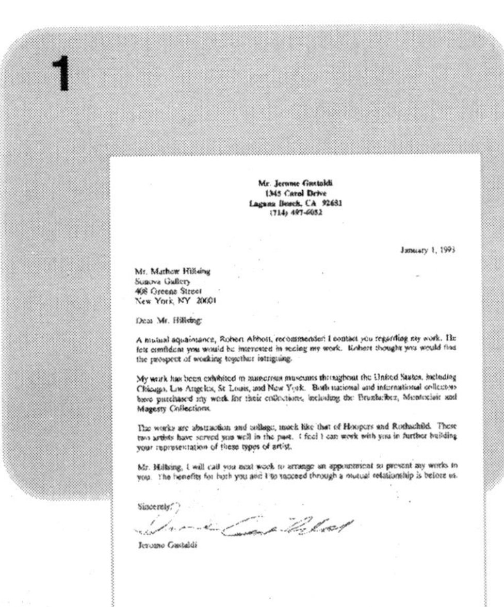

Mr. Jerome Gastaldi
1345 Carol Drive
Laguna Beach, CA 92651
(714) 497-6052

January 1, 1993

Mr. Mathew Hilbing
Sunova Gallery
408 Greene Street
New York, NY 20001

Dear Mr. Hilbing:

A mutual aquaintance, Robert Abbott, recommended I contact you regarding my work. He felt confident you would be interested in seeing my work. Robert thought you would find the prospect of working together intriguing.

My work has been exhibited in numerous museums throughout the United States, including Chicago, Los Angeles, St Louis, and New York. Both national and international collectors have purchased my work for their collections, including the Brunkelber, Montclair and Magesty Collections.

The works are abstraction and collage, much like that of Hoopers and Rothschild. These two artists have served you well in the past. I feel I can work with you in further building your representation of these types of artist.

Mr. Hilbing, I will call you next week to arrange an appointment to present my works to you. The benefits for both you and I to succeed through a mutual relationship is before us.

Sincerely,

Jerome Gastaldi

2

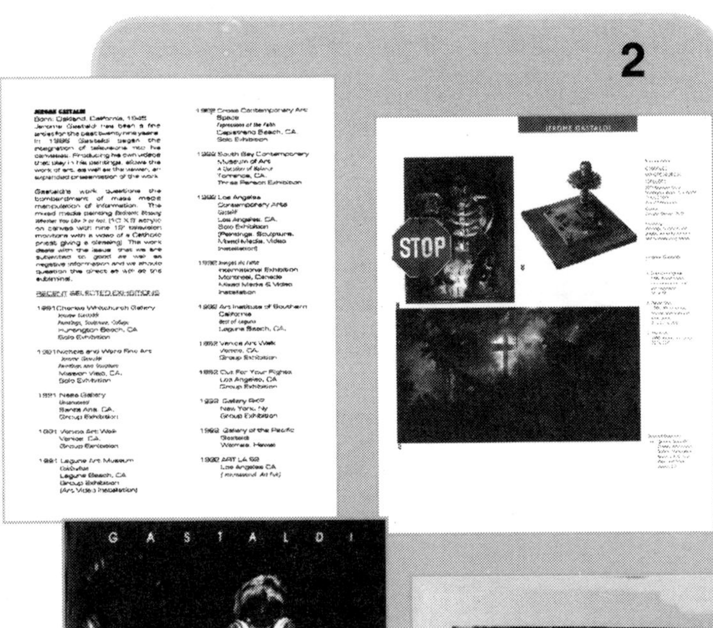

7

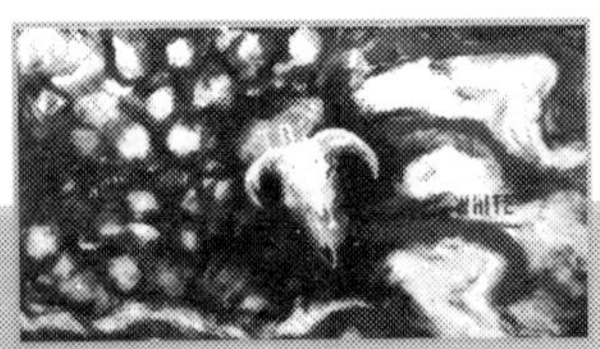

Around the Arts

EXORCISING THE DEMONS

Gastaldi's exhibit takes a concerned look at our times.

■ David Kopf

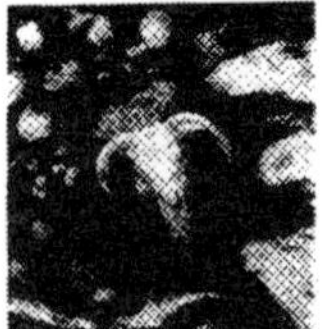

A work by Jerome Gastaldi
His work can be seen at the Charles Whitchurch Gallery

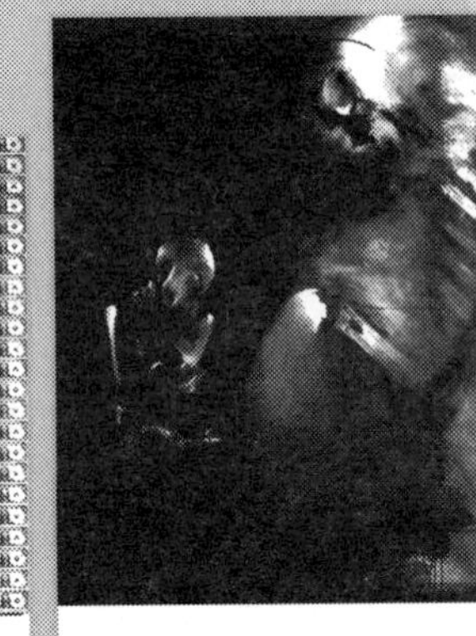

6

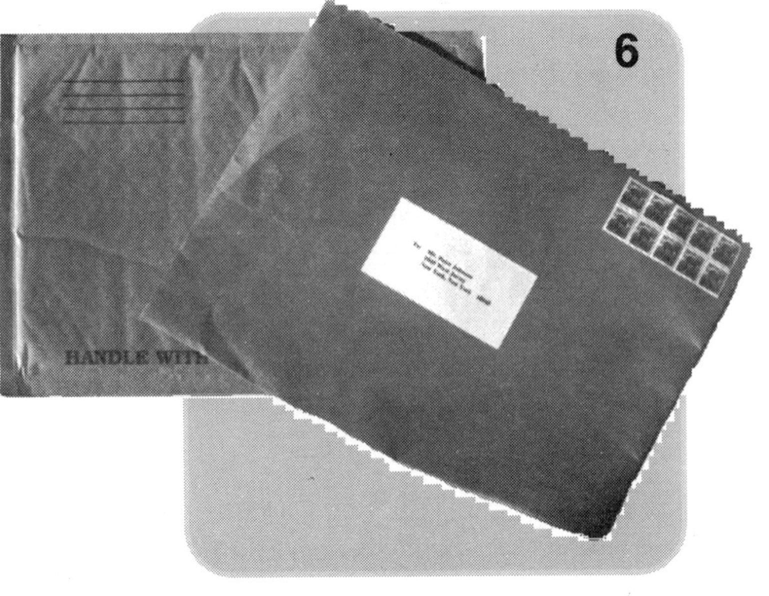

3

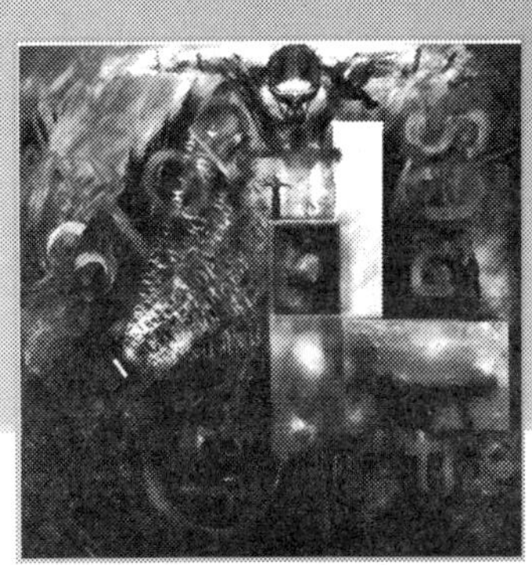

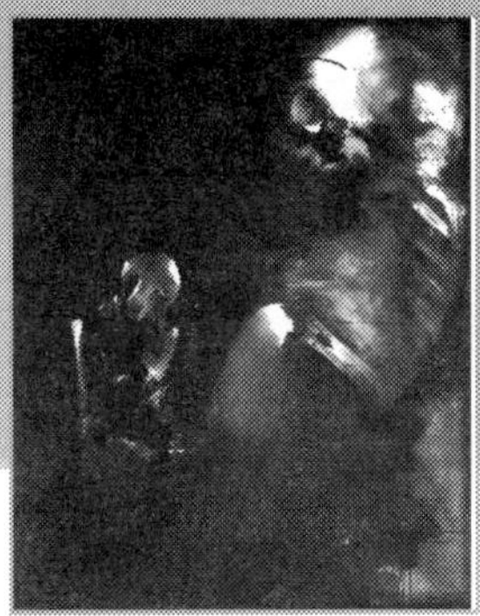

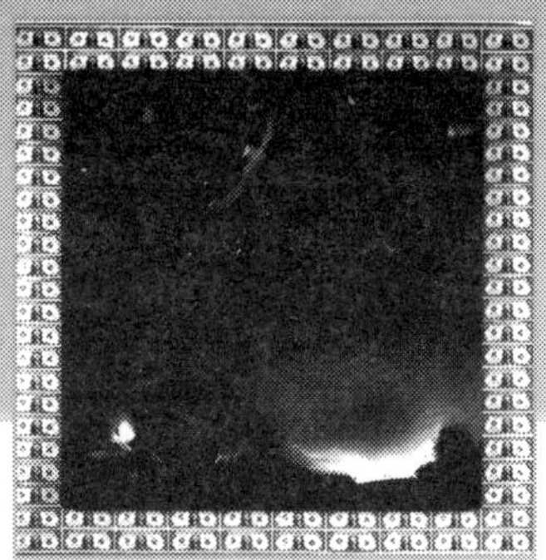

LABEL WITH NAME
AND DESCRIPTION,
SIZE AND DATE
ON BACK OF PHOTO.

4

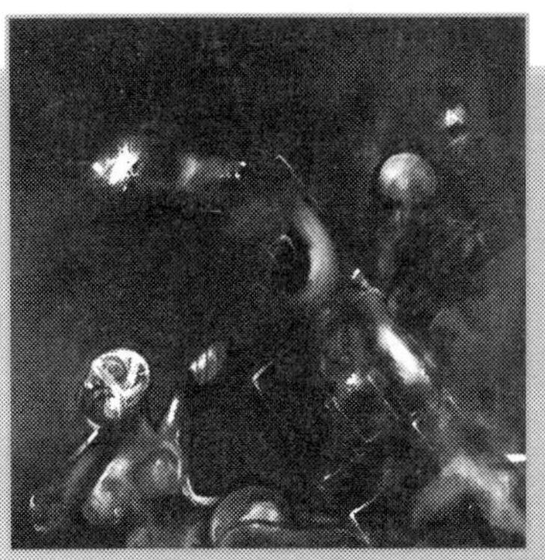

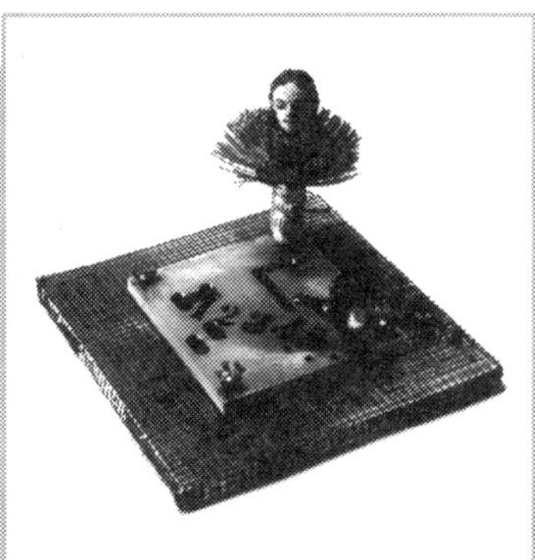

LABEL WITH NAME
AND DESCRIPTION, SIZE
AND DATE
ON BACK OF PHOTO.

5

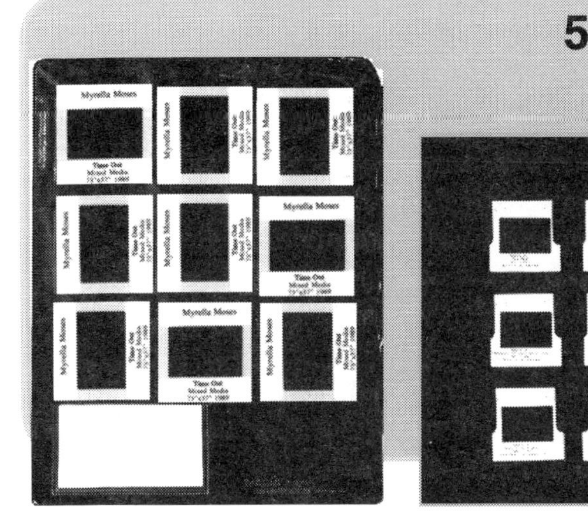

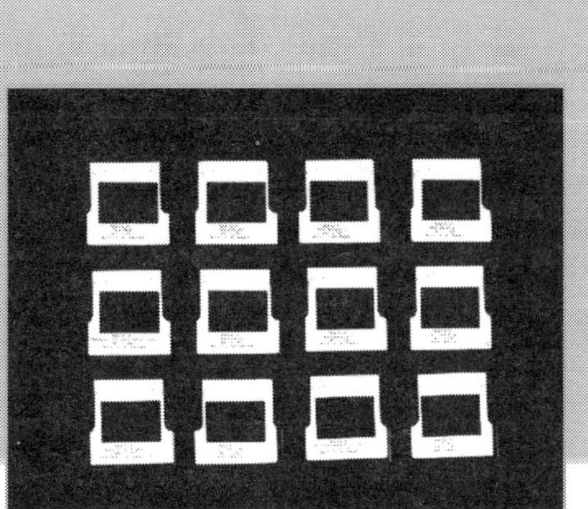

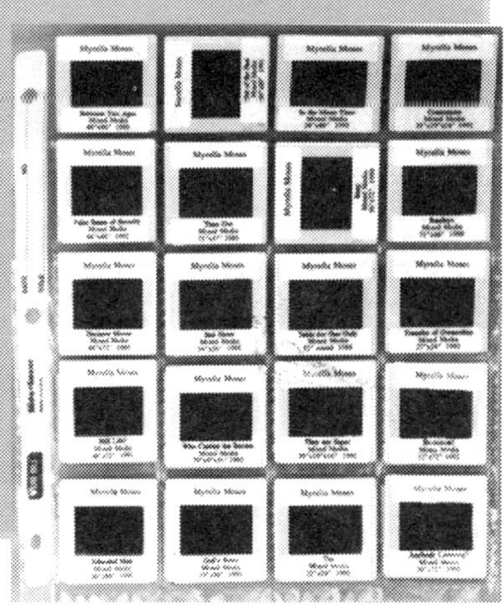

1. COVER LETTER
2. CATALOG, BROCHURE, TEAR SHEET, OR BIOGRAPHY SHEET
3. 3 PROPERLY LABELED COLOR 8 X 10 OR 8.5 X 11, PHOTOGRAPHS
4. 2 PROPERLY LABELED BLACK & WHITE 8 X 10 OR 8.5 X 11, PHOTOGRAPHS
5. PROPERLY LABELED 9, 12 OR 20 SLIDE SHEETS OF ALL PIECES SHOWN IN THE CATALOG BROCHURE OR OTHER MATERIALS
6. PADDED ENVELOPE AND SELF ADDRESSED RETURN ENVELOPE
7. OPTIONAL SAMPLE PRESS AND PROMOTIONAL RELATED MATERIALS

COMPLETE PRESENTATION

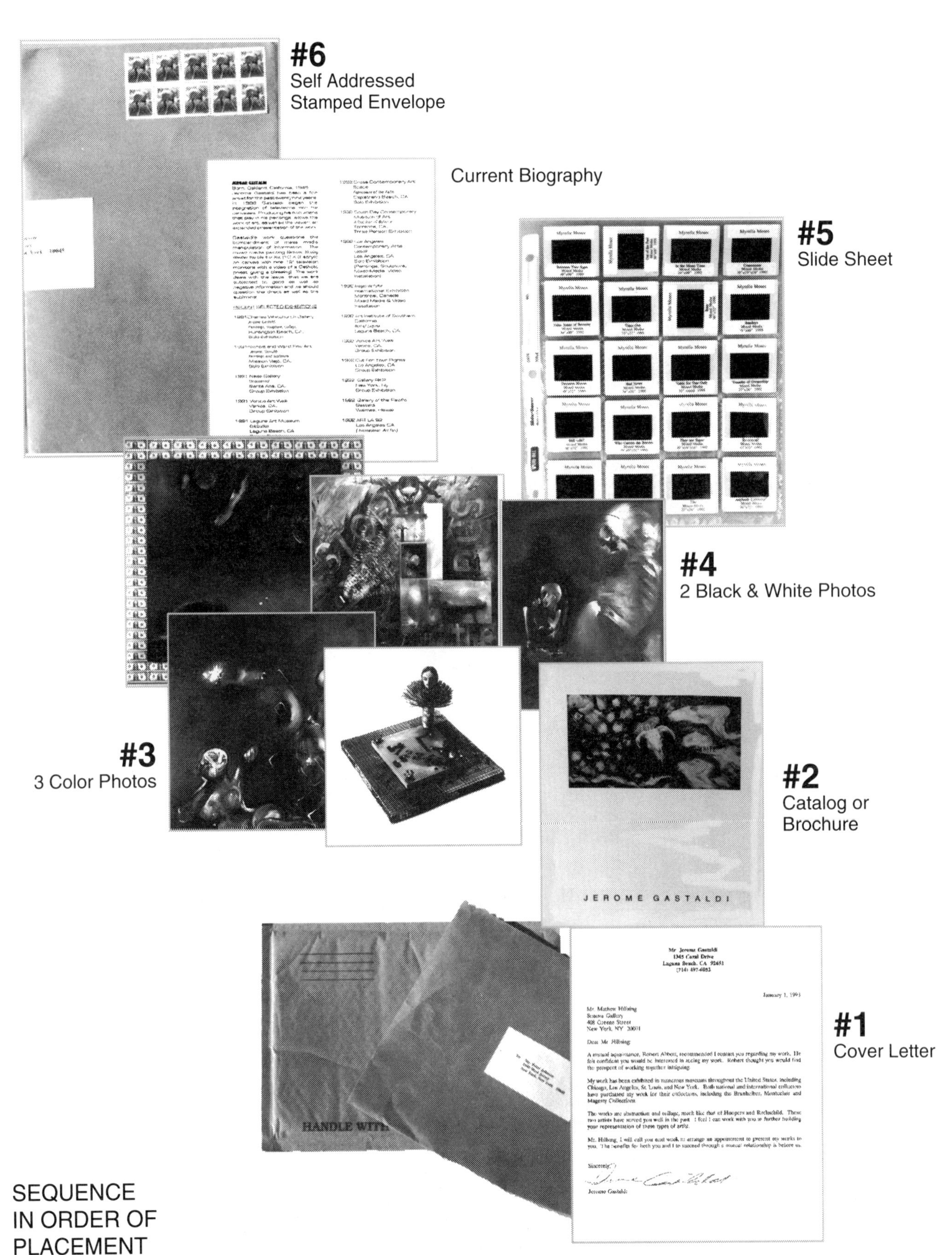

SEQUENCE
IN ORDER OF
PLACEMENT

Developing the Presentation Materials

The first portion of the archive that we will address is the academic presentation materials you will use to build your career. These are the materials you will use when soliciting your targeted markets. Remember, the emphasis on the presentation is academic, not commercial.

As the checklist shows, the presentation package consists of a cover letter, catalog or brochure, three 8" x 10" or 8-1/2" x 11" color photographs, two 8" x 10" or 8-1/2" x 11" black and white photographs, properly labeled slides of all images shown in the catalog or brochure, sample press releases, promotional materials ready to go to print, a self-addressed, stamped envelope for returning the materials and a padded envelope for the initial mailing.

Select the Works to Present

A complete presentation should contain images of your very best pieces. Choose pieces that are consistent with one another and convey your individual style and talent. Do not assume that by showing a variety of styles you are somehow demonstrating the scope of your skills. Such a presentation will only damage your potential for representation by its failure to indicate which of those styles is truly yours. Unless your current works have strong ties to earlier works, avoid showing the two together. ***Remember; if you want to be taken seriously, you must present a single body of works whose strength and continuity shows a well defined sense of direction.***

How do you go about selecting the best pieces to present? The first step is to pull out photographs or slides of all your current works. You should always photograph each work when you feel it is complete, to maintain a record for your archive. From this group, select those works which you feel are the strongest. Consider the availability of each piece for exhibition or for reproduction in a catalog or brochure presentation. If it has been sold and you do not have a photograph of the work, you must ascertain whether the owner will let you borrow it for photography or exhibition. Most will agree but a few will say no, so don't assume that you can use it. Always photograph your work.

If you do not feel secure in what you have selected, I recommend that you elicit the aid of a dealer, curator, consultant, knowledgeable art professional or our Artist Evaluation Service. Select someone whom you respect. Explain that you are developing a catalog and presentation materials and that you value his or her opinion. Most are willing to give you a moment of their time and their opinion.

Photographing the Works to Present

The next step in developing your presentation materials is to evaluate the type and quality of the photographs you have to use in presenting your work. The content, contrast, and clarity of a photograph is of the utmost importance in how well the image will reproduce in your printed materials. It is important that you do not cut corners with your photographs, as they will serve as your liaison to the art community. Pay very close attention to every detail about the image.

You may pay a professional photographer to shoot the images of your work, but this can be expensive. You may be able to find a quality photographer who likes your work and would consider trading photographic work for art. You may also consider contacting a local college or university, as there are always photography students with access to quality equipment who are willing to shoot your work for the experience. I strongly recommend that the student use a 2.25 or 4 x 5 camera. In those instances where your only alternative is to use a 35mm camera, make sure you are using a quality lens that will produce a crisp image, slow speed film and a tripod.

There are some basic guidelines to follow in photographing your works. The photograph is to represent the art piece alone, and therefore no other objects, animate or inanimate, should be present in the image. Avoid showing any ceiling lines or floor lines in the photograph, with the exception of installation shots. The size of a piece will be referenced when a label is applied, either to the print or slide, within the catalog or directly through installation shots. Paintings should be photographed unframed. Sculptures may be photographed with a background but you will want to ensure that the image is not too cluttered. The focus must be the art object.

Required Photographic Images and Negatives

Remember that you are strongly urged to photograph each art work you create. It is not necessary for you to have prints made from all your negatives. At a minimum, produce a 35mm color slide that you will properly label for all pieces, even those you will not be reproducing in your printed materials. For those that you will print, if possible use a 2.25 color negative or a 4 x 5 color negative or color transparency.

One 8" x 10" or 8-1/2" x 11" glossy color print should be made for each of the three strongest images among those you have selected to present in your package. One 8" x 10" or 8-1/2" x 11" glossy black-and-white print should be made from each of two additional images. Keep in mind that with black-and-white photographs, the contrast intensity is of utmost importance for quality reproduction in printed materials. The black-and-white prints will be used in press and promotional materials, so you will want to put your best foot forward with images that reproduce clearly for print. In total, you will need to print five copies of each image; one for each of the four presentation packages you will prepare and another for your master archive.

Keep in mind that before you go to print with any of your images, be confident about your selection. Once you set the printing process into motion, you are spending precious dollars.

Compiling Your Presentation Package

Assembling an academic presentation package is simple. You have already selected and photographed your very strongest images and are confident your selections are correct. Now you will begin preparing the other materials to complete your presentation package.

Cover Letter

The first item in your package is the cover letter. This letter will lie on top of all the other materials in your package. It is a letter of introduction and request that is personalized for each person to whom you are soliciting. You will never receive the desired results from an impersonal "one-size-fits-all" cover letter.

All your printed materials should be laser printed using a clean, contemporary font style. Avoid italic, gothic, and the like, which will detract from the simplicity of the presentation. It is not acceptable to present a package with a handwritten cover letter. A typed letter is adequate, but the impression that a laser-printed letter creates is invaluable. You may not be fortunate enough to own a computer with a laser printer, but in this technological age, access to one is easy. Check with your local copy shop, mail box shop, or office-supply store, as many of these outlets provide computers and even operators for people such as yourself. Refer to the chapter "Written Communications" for assistance in writing your cover letters.

Catalogs and Brochures

Inserted after the cover letter will be your catalog or brochure. Again, the purpose of the catalog or brochure in your presentation is to elevate your importance as an artist and the importance of your work in the art community. Because art images reproduced in print are usually taken more seriously, the catalog adds to your credibility. Make very sure that the catalog or brochure enclosed in your presentation package is not marred, dog-eared, or written in. It must be pristine. Again, it is the first impressions of your catalog that will really make a positive impact.

Even given the importance of the catalog, if you have the opportunity to present your work prior to finishing your catalog, by all means make the presentation. Let the recipient know that a catalog of your works will be available shortly. Keep the continuity of the presentation as if you already had a catalog using either twenty, twelve, or nine images. Be sure not to refer in your cover letter to the catalog or brochure as an enclosed item. Keep working to complete the catalog or brochure as soon as possible. Refer to the chapter "Catalog Design and Development" for the details of how to design and print your own catalog.

Prints

Following the catalog or brochure are the three color 8" x 10" or 8-1/2" x 11" prints. If you are not providing a catalog, the prints should follow the cover letter. After the color prints, enclose the properly labeled 8" x 10" or 8-1/2" x 11" black-and-white prints. Use the same label format as that for the color prints. **Every print or slide enclosed in your presentation packages must be properly labeled**. Never send out an image that is not properly identified. Each print should be labeled on the center of its reverse side. Again, handwritten labels are not acceptable. Typed labels are adequate, but laser-printed labels are preferred.

Laser-printed labels are available at any office stationery supply store. A good label size for prints is a 1" x 2-5/8" label. The format of information on a label is: first line -- artist name; second line -- the name of the piece; third line -- the media used; fourth line -- the dimensions of the piece; and fifth line -- year the piece was created. In designating the dimensions of a painting, state height by width; for a sculpture, state height by width by depth. For an art piece that does not have a title, use the phrase "Untitled" on the second line.

Avoid including your address and phone number on your print or slide labels. Printing demographic information about the artist on a label can turn the academic presentation into a commercial presentation. Any time you use your demographic information on printed materials, galleries may hedge on using your works. They may perceive you as trying to use their venue to acquire collectors and believe that you may be more than willing to go around the gallery directly to the collector.

Slides

Following the black-and-white prints are the 35mm color slides. Each slide is to be individually labeled with a laser-printed label. The format for the slide label is identical to that of the print label but the size is reduced. I have used a laser label that is 1/2" x 1-3/4". The print size must be reduced from a standard 10- or 12- point type down to 6-point type, keeping the same clean, contemporary font style.

Apply the label to the bottom front of the slide jacket. If you have an image that must be viewed with the slide on its side, purchase small arrow applicates and apply one arrow facing the correct way to indicate change of slide positioning. Keep the arrows small.

The slides must be inserted into a clear plastic slide sheet in the same order as the images appear in the catalog. Use only slide sheets that hold the exact number of slides you are presenting: for example, a nine-slide sheet when presenting nine images, a twelve-slide sheet when presenting twelve images, and a twenty-slide sheet when presenting twenty images. Never use a slide sheet where there will be any open slots, because it suggests that something is missing or was removed from your presentation.

Press and Promotional Materials

The next element of the presentation package is not required but can be beneficial. These are the press releases and promotional materials. Make sure to send materials that reference the type of venue you are soliciting. For example, send a gallery the press release from a gallery or a museum. Send the museum materials which are more related to academic events.

Self-Addressed, Stamped Envelope

The final piece of the presentation materials is not directly related to your art work but shows consideration to the recipient. Enclose a self-addressed, stamped manila envelope for the purposes of returning your presentation materials. If you do not enclose one, you may never get the package back. These packages cost money to put together, so you will want to get them back from each presentation.

Assembling the Presentation Package

Place each of the items within your presentation package one on top of the other, with the cover letter on top and the return envelope on the bottom. Make sure each is facing up in the same direction. Using a padded manila envelope large enough to hold the materials, slide the package into the envelope bottom edge first. You want the recipient of your package to pull out your materials seeing the top of your cover letter first. The package should have enough substance so that it cannot be bent. You may wish to insert a piece of clean, precut cardboard on both sides of your materials. Seal the envelope securely.

Address the envelope using a laser-printed or typed mailing label. Properly address the label with name of the recipient, his or her title, name of the gallery (museum, etc.), and complete address with zip code. If you are in doubt about any of the information on your label, call to verify. Ensure that a return address is clearly marked on the envelope. Purchasing a rubber stamp or stickers that indicate "Photographs Enclosed -- Do Not Bend" is a good idea to help further protect the package.

The presentation materials are then complete and ready to be sent to your qualified target person. You will need to have more than one presentation package available to send at a time. Prepare at least four complete duplicates of your master presentation package, or more if you are going to be soliciting more actively. Keep track of who has each of your presentation packages. Create a tracking system for yourself so that you can ask for the package back when the recipient has finished reviewing your works. Refer to the chapter "Presenting Your Work" for further information on properly presenting your materials and for keeping track of who has what.

Important Note: never lend out your master presentation package. The master package is used to make duplicates from but never for actual presentation. If you were to lend it out and not have it or your other materials returned, you would have to start over again.

The Archive

The master archive is the chronological record of your development as an artist. The archive consists of all your presentation materials, resumes, promotional materials, invitations, newspaper and magazine reviews, referral letters, slides, transparencies, and photographs.

Developing a complete archive is an easy process but one that requires your conscious effort to keep track of what is being written about you and by whom. As a new piece is photographed, a newspaper review (good or bad) comes out, or an invitation for a show is printed, it should go immediately into your archive. Always try to obtain a number of copies of each piece. The archive becomes a portable storage place for the chronology of your development as an artist.

A great deal of the materials in an archive are under your direct or indirect control. For example, the invitations, press releases, promotional materials, referral letters, photographs, and slides are either initiated by you or by the gallery or museum. You will be staying in close communication with your gallery or museum contact, and, therefore, will be aware of all written materials they are producing. The only materials in the archive that will require your diligent efforts to locate are the printed reviews of your work in newspapers or magazines.

For the artist who believes that he or she does not have the time or resources to dedicate to tracking newspaper and magazine writings, there are a number of clipping services that can do this for you. These services track your name through any variety of newspapers and magazines and then provide a copy of each article they find. The fees for a clipping service vary widely depending on the level of research you wish them to pursue. Contact an advertising agency in your area for clipping service referrals.

The Binder

The archive should be assembled inside a standard school-style notebook. You may wish to purchase a white, clear-view binder with a minimum of 3 inch rings, inserting an enlarged black and white reproduction of your work for the cover.

All materials within your archive should be inserted into clear plastic sleeves. This allows you to remove items from your archive easily during a personal interview without repeatedly opening and closing the binder rings. The plastic sleeves keep smaller items, such as invitations, neatly together and keep larger items in place without damaging them with a three hole punch.

Organizing the Archive

The first section of the archive is the master of your current presentation package. Insert the materials into this section in the same order as for presentation. As you update your presentation with a new catalog or brochure and therefore with new prints and slides, keep this section current. The older presentation packages should follow the current master, complete and intact. The prior packages will be used as a quick reference to your development as an artist during a personal interview. It is important to keep on top of the archive materials. For example, those who write about you today are also working to build their own careers. In a few years, they may become important art writers. What they said about you in the past will then take on an even greater significance.

Academic Resume

The artist's academic resume is a complete listing of exhibitions, education, teaching experience, and any other pertinent information demonstrating your progression of development as an artist. Think of the artist's resume as being the art community's version of a job resume. The very first item on the resume will be the artist description you created in the chapter "Who are You?" but edited to read in the third person. Have four or five copies of the most current resume slipped into a clear plastic sleeve. Resume writing rules and examples are provided in the chapter "Written Communications."

Letters Received from Dealers, Curators, and Others

Letters received from dealers, curators, collectors, and critics can be very powerful testimonials to the importance of your works to the art community. A letter from a museum curator complimenting your art is a strong statement of how that curator perceived your work. As a matter of business, you should keep all incoming and outgoing communications on file. Complimentary letters from influential people within the art community should also be kept in your archive. Slip each letter individually into a clear plastic sleeve and insert it into this section.

Installation Photographs

Installation shots are valuable tools that transport the viewer from imagining your works in an exhibition to actually seeing your works hung. These photographs allow the viewer to imagine your works hung in their space. Make sure you have shots of shows and locations where your works have been exhibited. Include a few photographs of the openings of these exhibitions that show people viewing your work.

Photographs of Important People Attending Your Show

Your art will receive increased credibility and value by virtue of the company it keeps, both the artists who are hung alongside your work and by those who come to see it. If a known and respected individual from the art community takes the time to come see your works, there must be something of interest to him or her. Others in the art community will be sensitive to this.

Act as your own "paparazzi." When a person of importance appears at one of your art functions, graciously introduce yourself. Initiate conversation about their interests in the exhibition. Prearrange for a friend to shoot a few photos of yourself talking with this person. Don't forget to listen to what the person has to say about your work. This is where the importance of your appearing at all events associated to the exhibition of your works is exceedingly important. A successful artist will learn how to network. You never know who may be involved with any given venue and who could be a good contact for your career.

Remaining Materials

The remaining materials are those that you will constantly collect from each event in which you participate. These materials include invitations, press releases, all promotional materials, newspaper reviews both positive and negative, magazine reviews both positive and negative, brochures, tear sheets, and any and all other materials referencing you or your works within the context of the art world. Whenever possible, collect multiple copies of each piece.

Presentation Checklist

Presentation Materials: (see the visual images provided earlier in this chapter)

✓ Cover letter

✓ Catalog, brochure, or biography page

✓ Three (3) 8" x 10" or 8-1/2" x 11" color photographs

✓ Two (2) 8" x 10" or 8-1/2" x 11" black and white photographs

✓ Properly labeled slides of all pieces shown in the catalog or brochure

✓ Sample press releases and promotional materials ready for print (optional)

✓ Self-addressed stamped envelope

Remaining Archive Materials:

✓ An up-to-date academic resume (updated throughout your career)

✓ Letters received from dealers, curators, etc. discussing your works (positive or negative)

✓ Black & white installation photographs

✓ Photographs of important people attending your show

✓ Invitations to shows/exhibitions

✓ Press releases regarding shows/exhibitions

✓ All promotional materials for each show/exhibition

✓ Newspaper reviews of your works/shows/exhibitions (positive or negative)

✓ Magazine reviews of your works/shows/exhibitions

✓ Brochures, tear sheets, etc.

✓ Any and all remaining materials referencing you or your works within the context of the art community

CATALOG AND BROCHURE DESIGN AND DEVELOPMENT

As we have emphasized before, the catalog is an important part of your presentation. The purpose of the catalog is to elevate your importance as an artist and the importance of your work to the art world. The catalog adds to your credibility, distinguishing you from the masses. Art works and statements seen in print are often taken far more seriously than those that are not.

It is not uncommon for an artist to perceive the need for a catalog but to feel it is out of their financial reach. This is an unfortunate misconception. Following the standard rules for designing an academic catalog and comparison shopping the production services you will need, you can develop a professional catalog of your selected works with only a modest investment. But if you still feel your budget will not let you create a complete catalog at this time, consider a brochure like the sample enclosed with this book. The brochure uses the same elements as the catalog but in an abbreviated version, allowing you to produce an effective promotional piece on a smaller scale.

In this chapter, you will learn how to properly design both a catalog and a brochure. A mock-up guide is provided with this book. Paste in each element as you finish preparing it. Use it as an aid to understand fully each point of design discussed in this chapter. Use the finished product to help you obtain bids from printers, showing them what you are aiming to achieve.

The Total Catalog

An academic catalog or brochure should include the cover, the academic essay, the artist's statement, the art images, the artist's biography, and the catalog design and production credits. A biography of the author's credentials is optional but can demonstrate the credibility of your writer. Each element has its own specific design and production guidelines to follow.

The size of a catalog can vary depending on your personal preference, but it should still follow the twenty, twelve or nine image formulas. Avoid producing a catalog that is so large that it is too flimsy and oversized for the presentation package. Make the mock-up of your catalog using copies of your prints to get a feel for how the catalog will look when completed. Use the mock-up pages provided inside this book to aid you.

The Cover

The cover is the first impression a person will have of your work from the presentation package. The goal of a strong cover is to grab the attention of the people you are presenting to. You want it to grab their attention so they look further at your works.

The front cover is composed of an image and your name. The image you select needs to be a piece that represents what your art is about -- a strong, mature piece that embodies the essence of your work. A cover image may be black and white, but some artists believe that it is to their benefit to use a full-color reproduction on the cover for their work. When reproducing a color image, the quality of the color separations is very important in creating a clean, crisp image.

The black-and-white images in your catalog will be produced from black-and-white half-tones. If you are concerned that your art presents itself best in color, at least have a color cover. The costs of creating a full-color catalog are astronomical in comparison to the production of a black-and-white catalog. Since the catalog will generally be presented along with the remainder of the presentation package, the black-and-white images inside the book will be supported by color prints and 35mm slides.

There are a few instances when it is better to forgo using an image on the front cover. If you feel your choice of images is not strong enough, you can successfully create a strong impression with your name alone. For the purposes of marketing your art, no matter what your goals are, you want your catalog to jump out at the viewer as something they will want to further investigate.

Be careful how you present your name, with or without an image. You must remember this is an academic catalog and not a vanity piece. Your name should be balanced with the cover image and not be so large that it overwhelms the image or dominates the cover. The name should be in a clean, simple print, almost sterile in appearance. Avoid "fancy" or commercial print styles, such as italic or gothic. Never use your signature as your name on the cover of a catalog; it is too commercial looking.

The ideal method of binding the catalog is perfect binding, a technique used in book binding. Other binding methods can be used, but the benefits of perfect binding far outweigh the additional costs. The perfect-bound method allows you to print your name on the bound edge, giving it a professional appearance. Many catalog designers do not realize the value of having the name on the bound edge. When sending your catalog to institutions, this binding allows you to request that your catalog be filed in a university, gallery, or museum catalog library. The catalog can be easily alphabetized, referenced, studied, and pulled for researching possible future exhibitions. When you use other binding methods, you do not give yourself this option.

It is ideal to have your work associated with ***institutional*** exhibitions. This increases the credibility of your work because it will now be associated with these types of venues. If you have the opportunity to produce a catalog in association with ***a museum, college,*** or ***university exhibition***, do it. Investigate receiving funding aid from the institution for the purposes of publishing the catalog. If the institution cannot help you financially, someone from the institution may be able to donate the writing of the essay. Print the name of the institution on the bound edge of the catalog, following your name and the name of the exhibition.

Printing a ***gallery*** name on the bound edge is not always a good idea unless the gallery is willing to fund the catalog's production. Other galleries will be less inclined to use materials printed with the name of another gallery. A gallery, however, will be pleased to use a piece that is associated with an institution if it can benefit from the credibility that that type of venue creates. If you do produce a catalog with a gallery, you may ask the printer to print a number of the catalogs with the gallery's name on them and then a number without the name. This will make it possible to take advantage of the best of both worlds as you can use those without the gallery name for other venues.

When producing the catalog yourself, use the print formats pictured. Print your full name on the top left side of the bound edge and the name of the exhibition in the center. Catalogs produced in association with an institutional exhibition should have the institution's name printed on the bottom right. Balance the text as you would for the spine of any book.

Be careful not to include addresses or phone numbers anywhere in your catalog. This will quickly turn an academic catalog into an obvious commercial sales piece, negating use of the catalog in an academic setting. A gallery will be hesitant to use the piece with your address and phone number in it because it suggests that you might try to circumvent the gallery and go directly to the collector.

The paper weight used for a cover should be 10-point cover stock, also referred to as 100-pound cover stock. A heavy-weight cover and a relatively heavy-weight inside stock will give the catalog a feeling of substance. When someone picks it up, it will be weighty rather than soft and flimsy in your hand. A glossy stock will highlight the image printed on the cover. Use your preference, either a glossy or semi-gloss stock.

CATALOG COVER DESIGNS

1

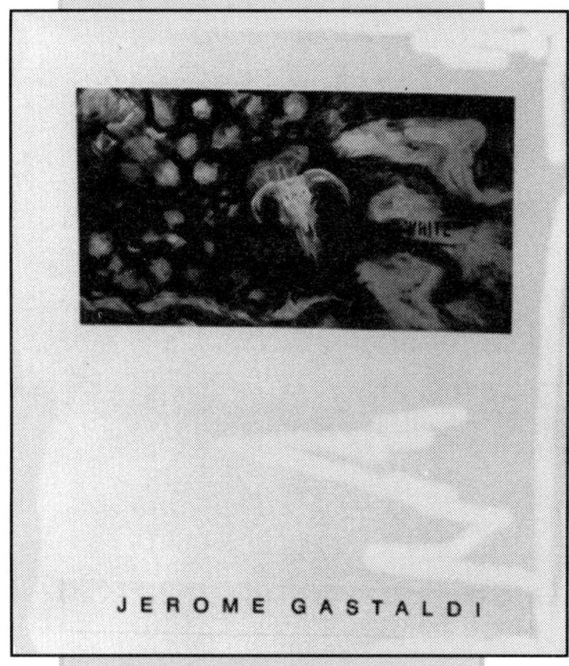

2

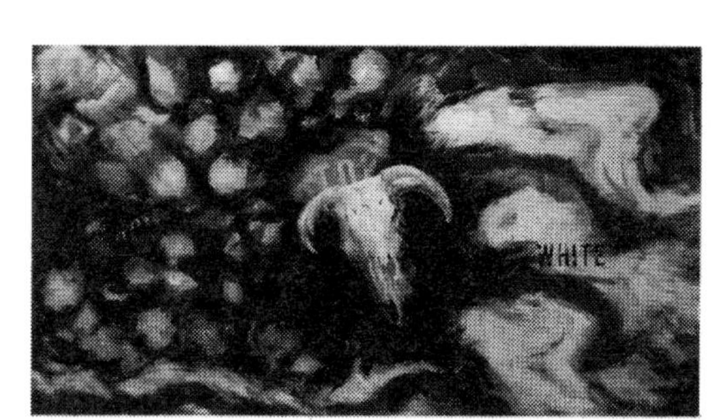

Gastaldi

3

CURRENTS

4

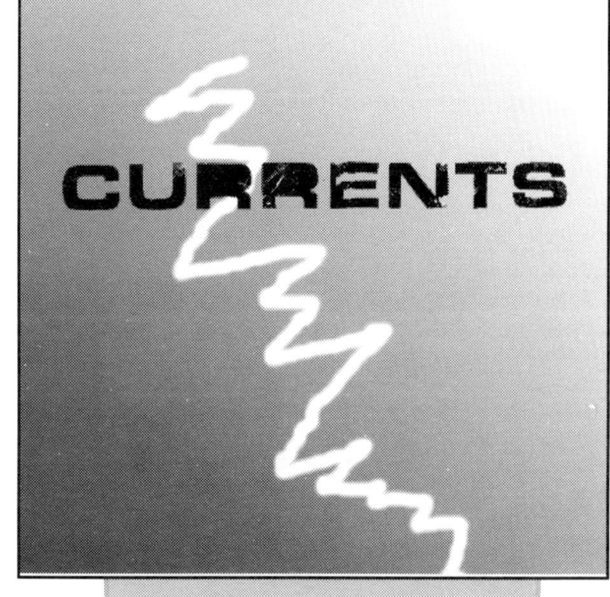

1 & 3 ACADEMIC SIMPLE DESIGN, RECOMMENDED
2 & 4 A MORE FLASHY LOOK, LEANS TOWARDS THE MORE COMMERCIAL LOOK

VARIOUS CATALOG SPINE DESIGNS

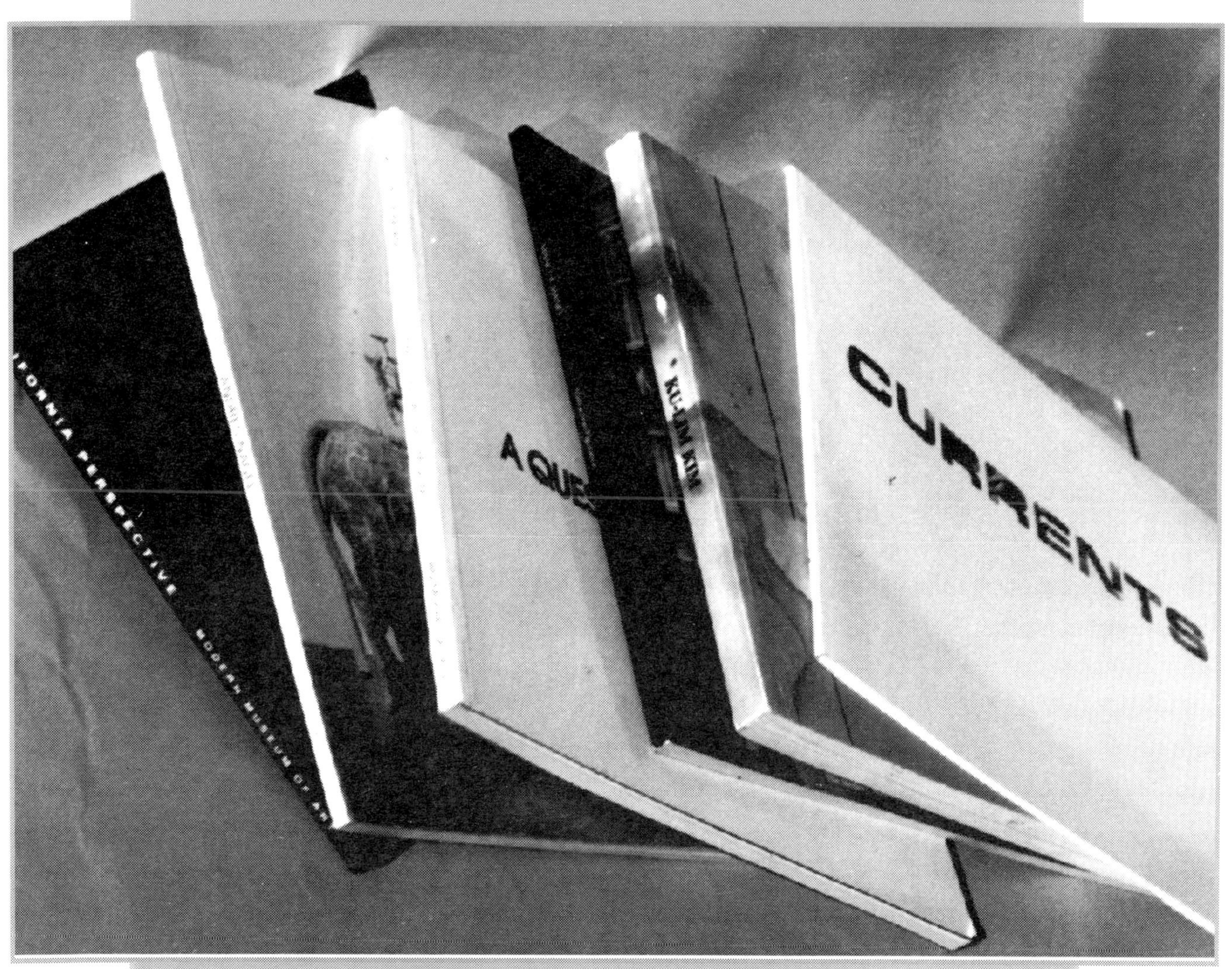

The Academic Essay

The academic essay is an examination of the body of works being presented in your catalog. Often the essay compares your works to those of historical artists in style, medium and message. The goal of an academic essay is to raise the credibility of your work within the art world and to create an understanding of your art in terms of contemporary and historical values.

Plan to hire a professional from the art community to write your essay: a college professor, an art dealer, a museum curator, or an art critic, for example. Select a person who is knowledgeable about your style of art and who has a strong understanding of art history in the context of your work. Interview each possible candidate making sure each likes your work and can see its place in the art world. You are asking your writer to attach his or her credibility to your essay so you want what is said to be positive but without undue hype.

Anticipate paying for an essay by the page or by the project. This is a given cost of producing your catalog. There are no set rate scales for reference, but the rate will generally increase with the increased importance of the writer to the art community. A 50% deposit to begin the essay is common, with the remainder of the fees due at the time of completion. You may also come in contact with someone who is interested in having some of their writings published. These individuals are more flexible with their rates and may even trade services with you for the opportunity to be published.

Spend time with the prospective writer. Talk about your philosophy in relation to your work, the message you are expressing, and so forth. Discuss why you have chosen to work in the style you do; what about this style allows you to express your philosophy, if you have one. If you have a life story that strongly influences your work, discuss it with the writer. For example, a Greek born artist I worked with was adopted by Americans and separated from her family at a very young age. She was told that her entire family perished in an earthquake. Twenty years later, with the help of the Greek Orthodox Church, she found her family alive in Greece. The experiences in her life heavily influence her work. Her art is so heavily colored by these experiences, it is important for the observer to understand these events. It is important for this artist to draw her story into her essay.

Be ready to work through a number of rewrites of the initial essay. Keep in mind the goal of what you are trying to achieve: to raise your level of credibility and importance in the art community. Be available to your writer whenever you are needed. He or she is going to put forth a great deal of time to create your essay and should know you are supportive of the effort.

Each author will have his or her own approach to writing your essay, but a representative essay may begin with a statement on your art style and philosophy including its historical counterparts and include a statement of what your work deals with. The next paragraph may meld the social focus into the historical use of your style of art by others. The essay may move into a detailed discussion of the historical use of the style in a manner that easily relates your work to the work of historical artists. The focus of your works may then be described using the same theme as the detailed historical discussion. The body of works may be reviewed piece by piece in the context of the historical reference. A good essay should close with a strong statement about the work.

An essay may range from two to ten pages in length within the format of your catalog. Do not allow the essay to become overly philosophical, thus losing touch with the reader. Stay away from the hype of a sales-type piece. The essay should create credibility for your work without overtly saying "its good." A commercial artist, however, may be more "slick" with the presentation.

The following is an excerpt from an essay written by Roberta Carasso, Ph.D. It is an excellent example of how an academic essay relates the artist's works to historical and social values.

ACADEMIC ESSAY SAMPLE

CIVILIZED UNREST

The art of Myrella Moses can be linked to those 19th and 20th century Western artists who recognized the value of Primitive art and incorporated its ideas into their creations. While having a similar affinity to the Primitive, a love and appreciation of the values it represents, Moses's art is not based on Primitive art, per se, but on the ideas Primitive art represents. Her art takes the Primitive legacy into the 21st century, where it becomes a focal point for humanity to reevaluate the substance of its life. Specifically, Moses's art confronts both the eradication of indigenous people from whose soul Primitive art emerges, and the effects the eradication has on all humankind. Hence, the exhibition deals with the undercurrents of unrest smoldering in all civilized people, including the indigenous.

The ideas in this exhibition far exceed the making of art and are not limited to the aesthetics of Primitive art that captivated artists of the past. This art takes a broader view, and looks at a phenomenon never considered by those who glorified the Primitive -- that indigenous peoples are vanishing and could, eventually, become extinct. In this regard, Moses's concern for the essence of the Primitive returns the art to the very foundation the Primitive art makers had in mind--that art is a vehicle through which life's values are crystallized.

Primitive Art extended significantly the known artistic vocabulary of the past two centuries. It yielded a far richer artistic palette which, directly or indirectly, affected many subsequent artistic movements, amongst them Cubism, Fauvism, German Expressionism, Surrealism and even Futurism.

Artists such as Pablo Picasso, Andre Derain, Constantin Brancusi, and others were drawn to the Primitive, primarily the African aesthetic, but also the arts of the South Pacific, South America, and Asia. They saw in the Primitive a freshness and simplicity, devoid of modernism and mechanization. The absence of individual artistic expression was innocent and unpretentious, yet, in its way, highly sophisticated in inventions and uses of form and space. The Primitive provided 19th and 20th century artists with both a freer range of expression and a completely new turn to explore in the artistic road.

Not founded on Classical Greek and Roman aesthetics, nor Judeo-Christian values with their hard and fast traditions of composition, design and perspective, Primitive art in general, and African sculpture in particular, had different origins. Western art was based upon a material view of life-the depiction of realism, the portrayal or glorification of an individual or event. Most significantly, it involved the creation of an object separate from daily life -- an idol to worship, a painting to be hung in a church or on a drawing room wall, a statue to be set apart in a palace, home, park, or museum.

African art, of that time, was an expression of the nonmaterial, the spiritual. It did not portray likenesses, nor recreate historic events, nor was it part of any artistic movement. It paid homage to ancestors, placated spirits, preserved values and beliefs, and was a reminder of morality and divine order from generation to generation. This dissimilar raison d'etre produced a complete unexpected look that was truly a revelation for the Western artist.

For example, Western sculpture was largely carved. Primitive art combined carving and assemblage. Shapes might be distorted, exaggerated, and even abstracted. A work might combine natural materials, such as straw, shells, etc. or was crafted meticulously from the finest metal. Often forms were large and airy, and it was not uncommon to omit or repeat facial details, place them in surprising ways, or redesign a face or an entire body. Also, Western forms adhered to principals of perspective and dimensionality, a throwback to a Classical era. Physical features might, on occasion, be distorted, but only to convey a more realistic look.

The Primitive sense of form and space was unencumbered by the weight of a vast and prestigious art history. A work could hang, designed to be seen from its side, its front, its back, or to be look down upon. Art was even designed to be worn. This freedom to use materials, form, and space in a less constrained fashion, coupled with a foreign aesthetic of tribal people, inevitably furnished Western artists with a fresh supply of creative possibilities.

Moses's art, too, is born out of an affinity for Primitive as a whole, not of specific culture. Elements of many cultures may be incorporated into one work -- American Indians, Africans, Amazonians -- all vanishing indigenous peoples. The art transcends culture in order to present an amalgamation of the human spirit, characteristic of people in danger of losing their past, their land, their languages, their way of life, their very reason for existing. Moses's art confronts the definition and limitations of the concept of primitive in its many aspects -- aesthetic, sociological, and political -- and demonstrates that Modern Man is the most primitive of all.

The art in this exhibition seems to move in three general directions, dealing with similar issues from different vantage points. Moses calls the first theme Primal/Tribal/Global. The second she labels Primary Interiors. Primal/Tribal/Global are statements about human nature through primitive motifs -- brown-skinned figures adorned with remnants of a tribal culture. They are mixtures of painting and sculpture, tending more toward the sculptural. Primary Interiors have a completely different look. They are of residues from human activities either in a bed, at a table, or in a chair. Moses chose these particular pieces of furniture because they are dominant settings for most modern human activities -- sleep, birth, work, and death. Then there is the third type of work. These combine elements of both the Primal/Tribal/Global and the Primary Interiors, where ideas are juxtaposed -- the modern with the Primitive -- and contradictions alongside similarities.

Primary Interiors are often large, white wall hangings. They are what Moses labels the Now. The Primal/Tribal/Global Moses refers to as the Then. Both are political, symbolically depicting the human dilemma and the impasse it inevitably reaches when the values it lives by no longer suffice. The impasse the art reveals is frequently the juxtaposition of two opposing forces that cannot find resolution within the confines of their narrow perceptions. The dawn of a new century, sparked by issues of rampant tribal holocaust is, therefore, the dominant subject of this exhibition.

Primal/Tribal/Global looks at the course that colonialism and technology set, and the consequences that result. The art deals with the effect of imposing values and life styles on people who maintain their own unique set of values and styles of living. Inevitably, this imposition has led to devastating consequences.

In (#17), "Educated Man from The Motherland," for example, a lone, surviving warrior stands, imprisoned in an era where technology has become a behemoth, too large to take on in battle. The warrior views the scene, bedecked in plaited hair Moses herself had worn, feathers, and Tibetan beads. He carries his bow, but no arrows remain. The fight is over. Despite his dignity and the respected rank he must have held among his people, he is a misfit in a modern world. He remains a warrior (translated from the American Indian as The One Who Carries the Burden of His People) but now he is just a curiosity. His way of life has slowly left him. He observes the cityscape, its lights covering the countryside like a giant organism. His once sacred landscape is no more. Looking out at the now electronic holy ground, he holds his bow, but his head is lowered. Is grief all that remains? The Moon, a constant witness to the ever-changing Earth, looks down. Perhaps it holds an answer.

Probably because of its size and powerful symbolism, one of the most noticeable works in the exhibition is (#14), "The One who Carries the Burden of His People." It is of a large, standing warrior merging with a wall. The brown-green color of the side indicates that the warrior has come out of rich soil, when the Earth was naturally productive. He steps out of the past, characterized by a sandy base, and disappears into civilization, represented by the gray, granite-like wall. Very much alive, he moves into the wall with the same dignity of bearing he held when he roamed the Earth freely. He, too, carries his bow, and there are no arrows.

Included in the work are a variety of plants, fish teeth from the Amazon, and animal bones. These natural elements provide an authenticity that intensifies the contrast between the ancient and the modern, the primitive and the civilized. These objects also demonstrate that Moses is not concerned with capturing a realistically depicted scene. Rather, she employs a mixture of symbolic elements to convey the spirit of all indigenous people.

To complete the art, bringing home the idea of the callousness in which societies vanish, Moses places at the feet of the warrior a discarded rear-view mirror, minus the mirror. This misshapen form was carelessly left on a street. Perhaps it just fell off a car. Perhaps it is the result of an accident. But in either case, it symbolized the carelessness with which modern civilization destroys and leaves things to rot. The rear-view mirror, when lying on the street, was the residue of an event. When placed at the warrior's feet, it represents modern humanity's flagrantly wasteful use of discarding of things, often leaving them helter-skelter all over the planet, and now in space as well.

The consequence of this carelessness is the disappearance of a tribe that was founded on harmony with nature and the continuity of the Earth and the planets. The omission of the glass from the mirror symbolizes the absence of looking back at the past and appreciating what the past has to offer. The rapid demolition of Primitive tribes results from neglecting to look in the mirror of these people....

Academic Essay Worksheet

The importance of selecting the proper writer for your essay is great. Talk to the prospective writer, considering each of the points mentioned below. After your conversation, complete this worksheet. Use your responses to determine whether this is the best person to write about your works. Make additional copies of this worksheet, one for each candidate.

Name of Prospective Writer: *Catherine Kingston*

Address: *5504 Broad St.*

City: *Los Angeles* **State:** *CA* **Zip Code:** *90046*

Telephone: *(213) 555-8910* **Facsimile:** *(213) 555-8920*

General Background of the Writer

1. What are the writer's credentials in the art community?

   Curator for the Contemporary Museum; PhD - Fine Arts

2. What is the writer's knowledge of Art History in general?
   ✓ Excellent __ Fair __ Poor __ None

   Explain:

   Extensive education in Art History - continuous involvement with academia in the art world.

3. What is the writer's knowledge of Art History specifically relating to your style of art?
   ✓ Excellent __ Fair __ Poor __ None

   Explain:

   Her personal pursuit is to show works which challenged current issues of their times. Art which may not have been so "comfortable."

4. Has this person written a published academic essay before?
Yes _✓_ No ___ For Whom?

Numerous for catalogs for her museum. (I have seen the auction catalog for last year's auction - well written in my opinion.)

(Obtain a copy of the essay, if possible.)

5. If the writer has not written an essay about your type of art before, do you feel the writer is willing to do the needed research to understand the style?
Yes ___ No ___ Explain

N / A

6. Does the writer have any other published writings?
Yes _✓_ No ___ About What?

She has contributed to a recent book discussing contemporary art and artists of the South Western United States.

(Read a few samples for their style of writing.)

7. Did you feel the writer was listening to what you were saying?
_✓_ Excellent _ Fair _ Poor _ None

8. Did you feel the writer was giving thought to what you were saying?
_✓_ Excellent _ Fair _ Poor _ None

9. Did you physically feel comfortable around the writer?
_ Excellent _✓_ Fair _ Poor _ None

10. Could you comfortably work with this person to your satisfaction?
_✓_ Excellent _ Fair _ Poor _ None

11. Rank this prospect from 1 to 10 (10 being best) as to their qualification to write your essay.
1 2 3 4 5 6 7 8 _9_ 10

Impressions About Your Art

Give the prospective writer a personal tour of your works preferably in your studio, gallery, or museum, where they can get the full impact of your works or through the quality prints or slides you have prepared for your presentation. ***Important: you may wish to show the writer only those pieces that have been chosen to be included in the catalog so as not to confuse them with other phases or styles of your work not being presented in the catalog.***

Discuss your artistic philosophy, what each piece means to you in relation to your philosophy, your view of the importance of each piece, and the views of other respected art professionals (critics, dealers, curators). Provide any written materials or reviews the writer may find useful in creating your academic essay.

If the writer is on top of things, he or she will probably discuss the materials you used to create each piece, your style, and how that style lends itself to the expression of your philosophy. Listen to the writer's remarks about your works. You will select a person who is positive and understanding of your work. His or her impressions, good or bad, will come forth in the words they write. Carefully choose the writer for your essay.

1. What were the writer's comments about your philosophy?

   She understood my points of view regarding the media's impact on society and social issues - she didn't always agree but was receptive.

2. What were the writer's comments about your art?

   She felt what she saw was strong, especially my use of strong color bleeds. She thought some were more mature than others - but good.

3. What were the writer's comments about your use of the styles and media of the art?

   Again, she liked my use of strong color and color bleeds. She thought I should experiment with raw canvases.

4. Did this person appear to have a comfortable knowledge of the styles and media?

   Very!! She was honest and straight forward, although sometimes brutily honest.

5. What were the writer's closing remarks to you as you said your goodbyes? Were these remarks positive?

She felt my work, especially as I mature, will have importance to the art community.

6. Rank this prospect from 1 to 10 (10 being best) as to their qualifications to write your essay.

1 2 3 4 5 6 7 8 _9_ 10

Financial Considerations

1. What was the writer's rate for the project?
_____ per hour __________ per page ___*$900*___ entire project

2. How does this estimate fit into your catalog budget?
__ Excellent _✓_ Fair __ Poor __ Not at all

3. Is the estimate within a negotiable range?
Yes _✓_ No ___ By how much are you separated? _____

4. Is the writer willing to negotiate this price?
Yes _✓_ No ___

5. Will the writer "trade" part or all of their writing efforts for a piece of your art?
Yes _✓_ No ___ (If yes, strongly consider the values being exchanged.)

Time Considerations

1. What time estimate did the writer give you to complete the project?

   3 weeks First Draft
   2 weeks First Rewrite
   6 weeks Entire Project

2. Does this time estimate meet with your needs?
   Yes ✓ No ___

   (Remember, you must be realistic in your expectations of how long writing takes. A good rule of thumb is to double your initial estimate.)

3. What other projects or jobs is the writer working on at the same time?

   She has just finished opening a new exhibition which will run for 2 months and has her next 2 exhibitions ready to hang. Less pressure for her during this time period.

4. Will these other projects interfere with the writing of your essay?
   Yes ✓ No ___

The Artist's Statement

An artist's statement is a brief explanation of your philosophy and message. This statement should be brief and to the point, and not so esoteric that the audience is lost. The use of an artist's statement in a catalog is optional. If your statement adds credibility to you as an artist, include it. In the same respect, including a photograph of yourself in the catalog is optional. Avoid using superfluous notes, poetry, diary pages, and the like. In an academic catalog, all these "personal touches" detract from the primary goal: advancing your credibility as an ***artist*** of importance to the art world.

Images

The images reproduced in your catalog represent the strongest selected body of works. You have taken painstaking care to select the proper art pieces, to have quality photographs taken, to select the strongest image of each piece, and to print the photographs with the utmost clarity and contrast possible. The next step is to assemble these images into your catalog.

The order in which images appear in a catalog is subjective. The image presented on the cover should be the strongest image in the catalog. Of the remaining images, print them in the order in which each image is referenced in the academic essay. Images representing art pieces specifically created in a series should be kept together in the order in which the series was meant to be viewed.

The actual images used in the catalog are reproduced from half-tones. A half-tone is the breakdown of an image from a black-and-white print into tiny dots. The half-tone is first produced from an 8" x 10" or 8-1/2" x 11" print of a 2.25, 4 x 5 or 35mm negative and then reduced to the size the image is to appear in the catalog, ideally, 5 x 7 or 4 x 6. Full bleeds where the edge of the image meets the edge of the page are more expensive but effective if you choose to use them. Whichever size you select, remain consistent throughout the catalog, avoiding jumping from one size to another to another.

The clarity and contrast of a half-tone is extremely important. A good lab will work with you to enhance the contrast of an image giving the image greater depth. Ask your printer to show you what can be provided in a half-tone and select the one that will best represent your work. Your lab may have some other suggestions as well. This is one area in which you can really shop the product.

Positioning the half-tone image on the page is critical. The image must appear balanced. Place the measured center of the half-tone directly on top of the measured center of the page. The borders around the image should appear equal; top equidistant to bottom, side equidistant to side. Use your artistic judgment and a ruler to ensure that the balance of white space around the image is proportional to the image: the greater the white space, the greater the perceived importance of the image. Consult with your art supply store for a good adhesive that will allow you to peel away the picture if your positioning is not quite right.

The images in your catalog will be positioned one for every two pages, as shown in the example on the following page. I recommend that you avoid presenting images where more than one can be seen at a time. The images will tend to fight with each other for the viewer's attention. As a general rule, place the image on the right-hand page. On the opposite page, print the complete description of the piece. A proper description includes the sequential number of the image within the catalog, the title of the piece, the media used, the dimensions, and the year it was created. Pieces without a title should be denoted as "Untitled."

The description is positioned to the left of the left hand page, approximately one inch from the edge. The sequential number is optional but can be placed on the measured center line of the page, with each item listed individually on lines below.

Another type of image that can be used in a catalog is the installation shot. The installation shot can give your work an institutional appearance, demonstrating the fact that your work is exhibited in important settings. The photograph you select should show the work in a museum-like setting, even if the picture was taken in a gallery.

TYPICAL CATALOG INSIDE PAGE DESIGN

7.
Cubes in Stainless Steel Frame
Carrara Marble, Stainless Steel
18" x 18" x 4"
1986

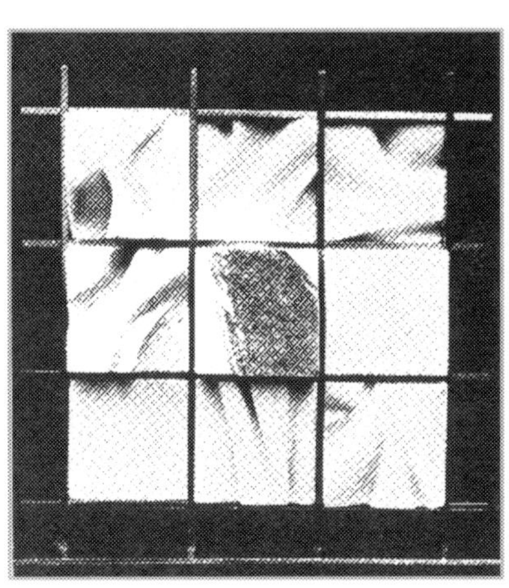

The Artist's Biography

The artist's biography is a selected listing of all institutional and gallery exhibitions of your work. Information about your education, teaching experience, commissions, and the like are not usually used in a catalog or brochure. The catalog biography is only a portion of your complete resume. List your exhibitions in chronological order, going back from two to five years. This will demonstrate your recent activities as an artist. If you have important experiences further back in your career, by all means, include those events in your biography.

Include in your biography all institutional events, gallery showings, juried competitions, or selected important benefit events. For the commercial artist, the biography will demonstrate that you are "out and about" in the art community as a viable commodity. Include the names of the institutions that have purchased your work for their collections. Private collectors are usually not listed in a biography unless the collector is someone of great importance to the art community. If you have only had a few exhibitions or collectors, do not worry. The essay will express the importance of your work for you.

The biography page generally consists of three parts: the general demographics regarding you, the artist; the listing of your events; and your picture, should you choose to use one. The layout of the page is rather simple. The first line is your name, often presented in capitalized letters. Spaced beneath your name is the phrase "Born:" followed by the year of your birth and the location, city, state, and country.

The title "Recent Selected Exhibitions" is printed below your demographics, often in capitalized letters. The list of exhibitions follows, using this format: year of the event, name of the institution or gallery holding the event, your name, the "title" of the event, and the city, state, and country location of the event.

You will want to present the information in as academic a fashion as possible. One-person shows that did not have a specific title may be referenced as "Your Name." Above all else, be honest with what you say in your biography. You can be sure that anyone seriously considering showing your work will check you out thoroughly.

At an international art fair, I met an artist who showed me his portfolio and biography. I was impressed by the list of venues in which he had exhibited his work, including those of a few director friends of mine. When discussing these exhibitions, he came out and told me he really did not show there. He had submitted his work to these people and felt it was all right to list them on his biography because they had images of his works in their possession. Needless to say, this was a misrepresentation.

The biography page is one good location for your photograph. Position the picture in the upper section of the page. Your personal photograph should be a simple black-and-white shot no larger than 2 x 3 or 3 x 4 inches. The artist's statement should accompany the photograph.

As your professional biography changes over time, simply create an updated biography sheet to slip into the catalog. The reader will see the progress you have made since the catalog was originally published.

The Author's Biography

The author's biography is a brief statement about the writer's credentials within the art community. This statement demonstrates the credibility of the author and therefore lends to the credibility of your work. Including the author's biography in your catalog is optional, and should be done only when the author's credentials are strong. Limit the author's biography to one or two paragraphs.

The Production Credits

The production credits are a way to recognize and thank the people who helped you produce the catalog. It allows you to support these individuals in the marketing of their services to others. The production credits are generally printed on the left-hand side of the last page. Include the names of the exhibition, the essay author, the catalog organizer, the layout designer, the exhibition coordinator or director, the catalog sponsor, and so on. Note: if any of these people are you, avoid crediting yourself.

Registering and printing the copyright notice for the catalog is important. Contact the Copyright Office of the Library of Congress, Washington DC, 20559 for information and guidelines for copyrighting published works. Consider registering your catalog with the Library of Congress Cataloging in Publication Division to obtain a nationally referenced catalog number for your book as a published work. Contact the Library of Congress for information and guidelines.

Brochures

Brochures are a viable option for those whose budgets do not warrant a full catalog. The brochure is a condensed version of the catalog. The catalog elements discussed earlier including the cover, essay, images, and biography are all included in a brochure. The rules for academic versus commercial materials still apply.

A sample four-page brochure has been included with this book. Notice how similar it is to the full catalog in form, content and function.

Tear Sheets

A tear sheet is usually a single presentation sheet which includes a brief essay, one or two images of your work, and a selected listing of exhibitions. A example of one type of tear sheet is shown on the following page.

The tear sheet functions in place of or in addition to the catalog or brochure. In the absence of a catalog or brochure, the tear sheet still gives you the opportunity to express the importance of your work with supportive images. Always support the tear sheet with the remainder of your presentation package, including photographs, slides and other materials.

JEROME GASTALDI

Representation:
FACT
Fine Art Communication Technology
775 W. 17th St.
Costa Mesa, CA 92626
(714) 722-6574

Contact:
Linda Rose

"Tel Aviv"
Is a hand pulled limited edition serigraph on 100% museum rag. Edition of 60 numbered prints, 12 artist's proofs and 8 printer's proofs. Completed in 1991.

This piece was completed during the Persian Gulf War. The face depicts fear and relief at the moment of impact.

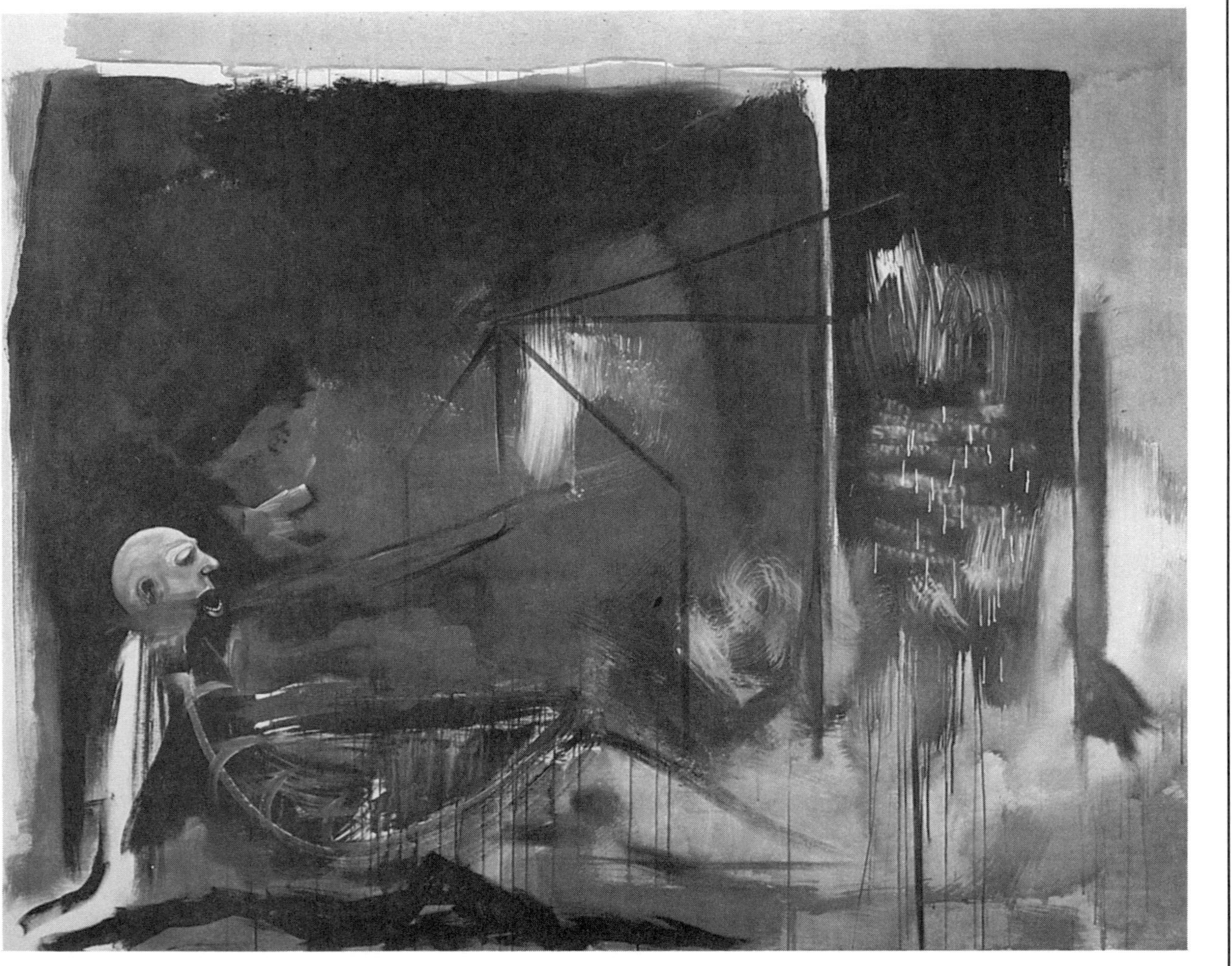

"Tel Aviv"
Original Serigraph
36" x 48"
1991

Catalog/Brochure
Bid and Budget Worksheet

Shopping the costs of the printing and production involved in creating a catalog or brochure is very important. Obtain bids from a minimum of four different printers before settling on one. The Contemporary Marketing Group will also provide complete service pricing on a variety of catalog designs upon request.

_✓_ Cover

Type of Cover:

_✓_ Color Cover
___ Black-&-White Cover
___ Name Only Cover

Bids Required:

_✓_ Color Cover -- color separations
___ Black-&-White Cover -- Half-tones
___ Name Only Cover -- Name Typesetting

Cover Printing Fees:

_✓_ Layout
_✓_ Cover Printing
_✓_ Printing of Inner Pages

_✓_ Essay

_✓_ Writer's Fee

_✓_ Images

_✓_ Black-&-White Half-tones (9/12/20)

_✓_ Binding

Type of Binding:

_✓_ Perfect Binding
___ Stapling
___ Other ________________

_✓_ General

___ Design Fee (optional)
___ Layout Fee (optional)
___ Word Processing Fee
_✓_ Copyright Fee

✓ Cover Color Separation

Vendor 1: *Star Photo Processing* Price: ______
Vendor 2: *Lindell Photography* Price: ______
Vendor 3: *A & B Photoprocessing* Price: ______
Vendor 4: *Custom Photo Processing* Price: ______

Black & White Half-tone(s) -- include inner images for this bid

Vendor 1: *Star Photo Processing* Price: ______
Vendor 2: *Lindell Photography* Price: ______
Vendor 3: *A & B Photoprocessing* Price: ______
Vendor 4: *Custom Photo Processing* Price: ______

Name Only Cover

Vendor 1: ______ Price: ______
Vendor 2: ______ Price: ______
Vendor 3: ______ Price: ______
Vendor 4: ______ Price: ______

Printing

Vendor 1: *Rebel Graphics & Printing* Price: ______
Vendor 2: *Canyon Printers* Price: ______
Vendor 3: *Southworth Printing Services* Price: ______
Vendor 4: *Readi-Press Services* Price: ______

✓ Essay

Writer 1: *Catherine Kingston* Price: ______
Writer 2: *Doug Weaver* Price: ______
Writer 3: *Richard Baylor* Price: ______
Writer 4: *Anthony French* Price: ______

✓ Binding Type: Perfect Binding

Vendor 1: *Rebel Graphics & Printing* Price: ______
Vendor 2: *Canyon Printers* Price: ______
Vendor 3: *Southworth Printing Services* Price: ______
Vendor 4: *Readi-Press Services* Price: ______

✓ General

Design Fee (optional)

Vendor 1: ______________________________ Price: __________
Vendor 2: ______________________________ Price: __________
Vendor 3: ______________________________ Price: __________
Vendor 4: ______________________________ Price: __________

Layout Fee (optional)

Vendor 1: ______________________________ Price: __________
Vendor 2: ______________________________ Price: __________
Vendor 3: ______________________________ Price: __________
Vendor 4: ______________________________ Price: __________

Word Processing Fee

Vendor 1: ______________________________ Price: __________
Vendor 2: ______________________________ Price: __________
Vendor 3: ______________________________ Price: __________
Vendor 4: ______________________________ Price: __________

Copyright Fee Price: *$20.00*

QUALIFYING YOUR TARGETS

You may be a professional artist with four or more years and thousands of dollars in education behind you or a part-time artist ready to take a shot at getting gallery representation. Or, you may be an artist in search of funding or a grant award to continue education or work. No matter what your activity, this is your chance to show the art world what you are all about, so do not underestimate the importance of doing your "homework." A truly successful artist understands the importance of planning their actions. Aside from your talent and the preparedness of your presentation materials, your knowledge regarding each venue you approach will put you on the right track, saving you time, money, and frustration.

The goal of qualifying targets is to find those galleries, museums and other venues that will most likely exhibit your works. A great deal of this homework can be done right over the phone. The key is to become as educated about the marketplaces you have chosen as you possibly can.

There are a number of fairly inexpensive investments you can make in yourself to have information and news come right to your door step. Join a local or regional arts organization. These organizations are very good sources of information about what is happening in your area, resources you can contact for services, discounts provided to the organization, and so forth. Many arts organizations are continuously providing programs for the further education and exposure of their member artists. I work closely with a number of large organizations and am impressed with the dedication of their leadership.

Subscribe to a number of the art publications. Select a few of the national or international publications, but don't forget to include those that report on the events and artists of your region. Your career plan may be focusing towards exhibitions around the world, but you must first walk before you run. Also keep abreast of your local and regional art events.

Read the reviews about the various exhibitions in your area. You may not agree with what they have to say or believe they know what they are talking about, but they tend to keep on top of who and what is happening now in their art community. Go see the shows they are talking about. You can use your visits for self-education, but always remember to make your own judgments.

Qualifying your targets will be most successful when you approach them in an organized, step-by-step fashion. As you begin to learn about the types of venues that interest you, doors will begin to open for you. You will be able to weed out those venues that are not of interest and focus your efforts to key targets. No matter what you are going for -- be it representation, exhibition, funding, or whatever -- it is imperative that you know as much about your target as you possibly can before presenting your work.

Create a List of Potential Candidates

The first step is to devise a list of the possible galleries, museums, and other venues in your targeted marketplace. There are many up-to-date books and magazines that list galleries, museums, and institutions with a synopsis of information about each. Check in your local public or university libraries, bookstores, and art supply stores for these publications. Numerous industry magazines publish yearly guides to the marketplace that are sold on newsstands. Pick one up when you see it.

You will find yourself inundated with names and places to research. Do not overwhelm yourself with an enormous list of candidates. As you go through the various publications, make two lists: an "A" list of venues of greatest interest and a "B" list of venues that appear not quite as interesting yet are possible candidates. Bypass any venues that do not seem to apply to you from the information they provide. The ultimate result should be an "A" list and "B" list of potential candidates to whom you will then methodically present your materials.

Learn How to Expand Existing Opportunities

If you already have dealer representation but would like to expand your market, try asking your dealer to help you in contacting other galleries. Most dealers have associates outside the community, but because of financial constraints, they rarely promote an artist beyond their geographical region. To make this proposition an attractive one to your dealer, prepare all the materials yourself, and offer to give them a percentage of your profits from the resulting outside sales. Most dealers will work harder for you knowing they are included in these revenues. The added visibility to your work as well as to the dealer should be worth the expense.

Call for Information

The next step is to gather information about the listed venues. "Teleresearch" questionnaires have been provided for this purpose. There are specific questions you will ask a gallery, museum, or institution. You will want to make sure your "ducks are all in a row" before you approach the venue for an appointment to present in person or by mail.

Complete a research sheet for each venue on your list. Keep them organized in the "Targeted Venues" section of this binder for current and future reference. These sheets will become part of your career plan materials. You never know when a person from one of your target venues will attend your opening. It is very important to be prepared for that spur of the moment opportunity when an important contact presents itself.

An opportunity for me arose right out of the blue. An artist friend asked me to contact a gallery in New York that had been interested in his work. He wanted to make sure that everything was on the up and up. I called the gallery and struck up a lengthy conversation with the director. We built a nice rapport over the phone. During the conversation it came out that I was an artist as well, even though it was never my intention to mention this. She asked me to send information about my art. As soon as we finished our conversation, I pulled out one of my presentation packages, went down to the post office, and express mailed it to her. It arrived in New York the very next morning.

I received a call the day it arrived. She was very pleased with the presentation and what she saw. In all her years as a dealer, she said she had never had an artist respond so quickly and so well to a request for information. An exhibition was booked and a contract transmitted back to me the very same day. (By the way, my artist friend also booked an exhibition with this gallery as well.) It is very important to always have your materials in order and ready to be sent out or you will probably lose out on a variety of opportunities.

When to Call

Timing is important when trying to create opportunities for yourself. You can use a few "tricks" to work a good teleresearch program. There are good and bad days to call people for information: days that are influenced by outside factors you can generally predict.

Many venues are closed on Sundays and Mondays. Therefore, use these days for something else in your plan. Saturdays tend to be very busy days for galleries, museums, and other venues as well as for their decision makers. Avoid calling on any of these days. Your goal is to speak directly to the person who makes the decisions.

Tuesdays are the day back from the weekend. This is a hectic day for taking care of business that occurred over the weekend and any "fires" that must be put out. Friday is a bad day also, because people are trying to wrap things up to get away for the weekend. That leaves you with Wednesdays and Thursdays. You are most apt to have the person you wish to speak to in on those days and their ear responsive to what you are saying. This is not to say that you must only call on those two days, but logic dictates that your chances are best on these days. Make your introductory calls on these days, and if directed to call on another day, put it in your calendar and do so. You have now started the ball rolling.

How Many Venues to Call

Only call as many venues as you are capable of following up on. If you start the communication with a venue and then are not able to follow up in a timely fashion, it will leave the impression that you are either not serious, not organized, or possibly not easy to work with. The best way is to make your calls until you have one or more contacts that fall into your plan or have expressed an interest in seeing your work. Follow up on your contacts the same day you call, using the methods in the chapter "Presenting Your Work." Once you have exhausted the possibility of working with a venue, continue making your research calls again until you have another active venue from your list.

Remember, you will not want to present to too many venues in the same area at one time, as word will get around that you are canvasing the area and are not selective. This may be perceived as an air of desperation on your part. Be selective about whom you chose to approach actively. You want to work with the best venues you are able to obtain. It is important to be prepared for the good and the bad, so keep an eye open for the "flakes."

Referrals and Rapport

Along with the goal of obtaining information, you will want to build a rapport with the person to whom you are speaking. If you were referred to this venue by an influential person, refer to that person within your opening statement. For example, ask whom you are speaking to what their name is and use it within your conversation. Speak clearly and with volume. A meek, mild voice will make the person on the other end feel you are insecure. The key here is to create a first impression and gather information from the other person. Anything that may inhibit your presentation needs to be corrected.

Thank You Is Always Appropriate

Once you have finished your conversation, thank the person to whom you are speaking. Be considerate and appreciative of the time, whether he or she chose to be helpful or not. Always be friendly and professional on the phone. You will find you will open more doors that way.

If you feel you are not ready, capable, or are simply uptight, you may have a friend or spouse do your talking for you. Preferably, select someone who is an extravert. A second party can expound on your good points without coming off as braggadocios. Remember to educate them thoroughly on your work. Run through the presentation with your representative until they have the presentation down cold.

Sample Conversation -- A Scripted Guide

Some people are not comfortable with making information soliciting phone calls. Don't be concerned; this is very common. For those people, I have "scripted" some opening lines that may be helpful. You can create your own personalized script to reflect your own personality. Remember, be professional.

> *Good morning (afternoon, evening, day)*
>
> *My name is* ________________________. *To whom am I speaking, please?*
>
> *Hi,* ______________________________.
>
> *I was referred to you by* __________________________ *(name of the referring party.)*

I would like to ask you about your ________________________ (venue type).

\- or -

Could you tell me about your ____________________________ (venue type).

If the person is agreeable to fielding questions at this point, you would begin with the questions following the demographic information that you have already obtained from one of the publications. Don't start out with "what is your address" or "what is your facsimile number." Use some of the questions that are more specific to the venue. You will want to get to the information that is important to you.

If the person is not agreeable to questioning, ask if there is a better time in which you may call back. You may even want to go so far as to set a time for a phone appointment or set an appointment for a personal presentation. Write the appointment down on your calendar, and be sure to keep it. Remember the old adage, "the squeaky wheel gets the grease." The more presentations you make, the easier it becomes.

Get Started

Now that you have the ground rules in mind, it is time to get started. The biggest step in becoming successful is simply to start working your plan. You will continue to work on this process throughout your career.

Once you have established relationships with a number of venues, you will hopefully become busy. The time you will have to devote to the process will lessen. Make appointments with yourself to continue the research and contact process, even if it is only one day a week. If you have someone who can help you stay organized and keep the process going, work with them to assist you to actively research new opportunities. It is important to always keep your "feelers" out. At some point, one of your venues may fall by the wayside and you will need to pick up the slack with another. It is best to have something already working rather than to have to start from scratch at that moment. Always keep tuned into potential possibilities for exhibitions. Keep on presenting.

CAREER PLAN

Teleresearch Worksheets

The following worksheets are designed to help you gather important information about the galleries, museums, dealers, and other possible venues you are interested in pursuing. There is a great deal of information that is important to you in deciding which opportunity to approach. Realize some of the information can be obtained in books and magazines; other information you will gather through your phone conversations. You may not be able to gather all the information in one phone call. As you learn more, note it on that venue's worksheet.

It is important for you to maintain a worksheet even for those targeted venues from which you receive negative responses. A future opportunity to work with that venue may pose itself, and it would be important for you to have a record of prior contacts for referral.

Make a number of copies of each type of worksheet for your research files. Keep a separate sheet for each targeted resource.

The information on each of these worksheets may be obtained from a number of sources in addition to your call. You may learn a great deal about a venue from magazines, artists and others. Use a variety of resources to gather the information you will need to make an informed decision regarding the viability of this venue for your work.

Teleresearch Worksheet: Galleries

Date of Contact: *03 / 24 / 93*

Source of Listing: *Personal*
Referred by: *C. Kingston*

Name of Gallery: *Gallery Winchester*
Address: *142 Spring Street*

City: *New York*
State: *NY* Zip: *10012* Country: *USA*
Telephone: *(212) 925-0001* Facsimile: *(212) 925-0005*

Owner/Director: Louise Winchester Title: *Owner*
Spoke with: *Allen Peth* Position/Title: *Assistant Director*

Gallery Hours: *T - F 12:00am - 6:00pm, Sat 10:00am - 6:00 pm*

What type of space is this?

✓ Gallery
__ Co-op
__ Alternative Space
__ Commercial Gallery
__ Gallery Chain
__ Other ________

What types of art are exhibited in this space? *Paintings, sculptures, graphic pieces*

What is the focus of the gallery? *Modern and contemporary artists*

Are these pieces:

✓ originals
✓ limited editions
__ prints
__ secondary product lines (t-shirts, etc.)

How large is the space? Wall footage: ________ Ceiling Height: ________

Are the works they exhibit limited to a specific price range? *$ 500.00* to *$ 5,000.00*

At this point, ask yourself "is my work appropriate for this space?" ✓ ***Yes*** __ ***No***

If "Yes," continue the conversation.
If "No," ask for a referral to another gallery.

Whom do they currently represent?

Keith Delphi
Jerome Gastaldi
Mary Ann Williams
Alfred Earle

__ Blue Chip Artists ✓ New Artists

Do they take on new artists? ✓ Yes __ No (If "No," ask for a referral to another gallery.)

What are their presentation policies? *Submit color and b/w prints, labelled slides (in sheets only), catalogs, print reviews, tear sheets and a current biography/resume.*

What are their slide review policies? *Materials reviewed on Wed's only. If works are liked, schedules an artist studio visit prior to accepting artist into the gallery.*

To whom should the materials be directed? *Louise Winchester*

Remember; if the venue is within driving range of your studio, deliver the presentation materials in person.

How long has the gallery been open? *10 years (this location 3 years)*

How often do they hold shows? *Every 2 months on an average*

What types of shows do they hold? ✓ Solo Shows ✓ Group Shows __ Other
✓ Group Shows of the Gallery Artists

Who/what/when are the upcoming events? *April - Jerome Gastaldi*
June - Cancer Benefit - Group Show Local Artists
July - New Artists Group Show

What are the customary promotions done with each show?

✓ invitations	✓ press releases	__ trade advertisements
✓ receptions	__ catalogs	__ tear sheets
__ brochures	__ fliers	__ posters
✓ literature	✓ other Interested in joint producing catalog of works	

Do they have a good rapport with the press? ✓ Yes __ No

Are they represented at art expos or important art events? ✓ Yes __ No

Do they have a reputation for building careers? ✓ Yes __ No

Sales? ✓ Yes __ No

Do they have institutional contacts with museums and others? ✓ Yes __ No

What is their policy regarding commissions for sales? *50/50 split after exhibition expenses have been recovered. Receive check within 30 days of sale.*

What is their policy regarding commissions for sales made through other spaces they book on behalf of the artist? *50/50 split with the other venue - 10% of the artists split is paid as commission to the Winchester Gallery.*

If you have the opportunity to contact one or more of the gallery's artists, ask about:

What kind of reputation does this gallery have? *Excellent - Honest with the artist. Shows well organized and well attended.*

Do they promptly pay their artists? *Monies are always recieved on day 30. Checks have always cleared immediately.*

Referred by this gallery to: *Caldwell Gallery, 89 Aster St., Chicago, attn: Camille Gallant*

Comments: *Good feeling about this gallery - have Andy visit the gallery just to see the layout this week. Get his feed back as to the quality of exhibition and space. Do my large pieces fit the space?*

____

____

____

____

Next Step: __ Appointment to present to: ____________________
Date: __________ Time: ______ Location: _______

✓ Mail presentation materials to: *Louise Winchester*

__ Call again at a future date (schedule it in your calendar)
Ask for: ______________________________

__ Not a viable gallery for you. (Why?)

Teleresearch Worksheet: Museums

*** ***Remember -- ANY museum you can get your work into is an excellent advancement for your career*** ***

Date of Contact: *03/24/93*

Source of Listing: *Personal*
Referred by: *C. Kingston*

Name of Museum: *Davis Modern Museum*
Affiliation: ______
Address: *621 Doyle Carlton Dr.*

Goal of this call:
✓ Piece in group show
__ Solo Show
__ Acquire for collection

City: *Tampa*
State: *FL* Zip: *33602* Country: *USA*
Telephone: *(813) 223-4680* Facsimile: *(813) 223-6680*

Director: *Duncan Lee* Curator: *Kennedy Benton*
Spoke with: *Andrew Marquette* Position/Title: *Assistant Director*

Museum Hours: *T - Sat 10:00am - 5:00pm*

What types of art are exhibited in this museum? *Paintings, sculpture, mixed media pieces*

What is the focus of the museum? *Modern and contemporary European artists (two local artist shows held yearly, September & January)*

How large is the space? Wall footage: ______ Ceiling Height: ______

Do they show contemporary or traditional artists? ✓ Contemporary __ Traditional

What type of artists do they show? ✓ Local __ Regional ✓ International

What artists are currently in their collection? *Newman, Mathews, Richards, Scott, Gastaldi*

At this point, ask yourself "is my work appropriate for this space?" ✓ ***Yes*** __ ***No***

> ***If "Yes," continue the conversation.***
> ***If "No," ask for a referral to another museum.***

What are their presentation policies? *Submit catalog, color and b/w prints, labelled slides (in slide sheets only), print reviews, tear sheets. A current resume a must.*

To whom should the materials be directed? _Andrew Marquette_

Remember; if the venue is within driving range of your studio, deliver the presentation materials in person.

How long has this museum been in existence? _5 years_

Do they hold an annual fund raising auction? ✓ Yes __ No

Will they accept donations from artists for the museum's collection? ✓ Yes __ No

What is their policy for donations to the museum? _Same presentation materials as regular submission only reviewed twice a year by aquisition committee._

How often do they change their exhibitions? _Every 1 1/2 months_

What were some of their past shows?
The Newhall Retrospective
Gastaldi, Newman and Resnick
ALS Benefit Auction

Who/what/when are their upcoming events?
June - Local Artists Show - Group
July - Art of the 90's - Group Show
July - 1993 ALS Benefit Auction

What are the customary promotions done with each show?

✓ invitations	✓ press releases	__ trade advertisements
✓ receptions	✓ catalogs	__ tear sheets
__ brochures	__ fliers	✓ posters
✓ literature	__ other ______	

Ask for a membership application and a current newsletter (so that you can see who supports the museum, etc.)

Referred by this museum to: _The Modern Museum of Art, Santa Ana, CA_

Next Step: __ Appointment to present to: ______
Date: ______ Time: ______ Location: ______

✓ Mail presentation materials to: _Andrew Marquette_

__ *Call again at a future date (schedule it in your calendar)*
Ask for: ______

__ Not a viable museum for you. (Why?)

Teleresearch Worksheet: Independent Dealers

Date of Contact: *03 / 24 / 93*

Source of Listing: *Hillsing*
Referred by: *Hillsing*
Goal of this call:
__ Piece in group show
__ Solo Show
✓ Representation

Name of Dealer: *Jordan Swift*
Address: *33461 Ascot Court*
City: *Los Angeles*
State: *CA* Zip: *90046* Country: *USA*
Telephone: *(213) 458-0095* Facsimile: *(213) 458-9095*

Spoke with: *Jordan* Position/Title: *Independent Dealer*

Gallery Affiliations?: *The Contemporary Works Gallery*
Stuart Koll International
Sonova Gallery

Institutional Affiliations?: *The Contemporary Museum*
The Davis Modern Museum
Southern California Arts School

What type of space is available to this dealer?
✓ Gallery __ Commercial Gallery __ Co-op
__ Gallery Chain ✓ Alternative Space
✓ Other *Museum & University*

What types of art do they represent? *Contemporary Artists-Painters, Sculptors, Photographers*

What is their focus? *Artists "On The Edge" - Contemporary Issues*

Do they work with: ✓ originals __ prints
✓ limited editions __ secondary product lines (t-shirts, etc.)
__ commissions __ others ____

Are the works they deal with limited to a specific price range? *$500.00* to *$2,500*

At this point, ask yourself "is my work appropriate for this dealer?" ✓ Yes __ No

If "Yes," continue the conversation.
If "No," ask for a referral to another dealer.

Whom do they currently represent? *Victoria Newman*
Torrell Darling
Hanson Bright
__ Blue Chip Artists ✓ New Artists

Do they take on new artists? ✓ Yes __ No (Ask for a referral)

What are their presentation policies? *Provide printed materials, color and b/w prints, slides and catalogs. Will review all materials.*

To whom should the materials be directed? *Jordan Swift*

How long has this person been in the business? *15 years*

What is their reputation in the art community? *Jordan is very well respected for working with and developing young artists. I had heard of his name and reputation well before receiving a referral from Mathew.*

How often do they hold shows? *Schedules 2 simultaneous shows per month - different venues.*

Who/what/when are their upcoming events? *Newman - Cont. Works Gallery - July*
Darling - Stuart Koll Internationl - July
Bright - Sonova Gallery - August

What are the customary promotions done with each show?

✓ invitations	✓ press releases	__ trade advertisements
✓ receptions	✓ catalogs	__ tear sheets
__ brochures	__ fliers	__ posters
✓ literature	__ other ______	

Do they have a good rapport with the press? ✓ Yes __ No

Are they represented at art expos or important art events? ✓ Yes __ No

Do they have a reputation for building careers? ✓ Yes __ No

Sales? ✓ Yes __ No

Do they have institutional affiliations with museums or others? ✓ Yes __ No

Do they open up opportunities for their artists with institutions? ✓ Yes __ No

What is their policy regarding commissions for sales? *60/40 split with the artist on all sales.*

What is their policy regarding commissions for sales made through other spaces they book on behalf of the artist? *Networks heavily. Same 60/40 split.*

If you have the opportunity to contact one or more of the gallery's artists, ask about:

What kind of reputation does this dealer have? ____________________

Do they promptly pay their artists? ____________________

Next Step: ✓ Appointment to present to: *Jordan Swift*
Date: 04 / 02 / 93 Time: 10:00 am Location: *Sonova Gallery*

__ Mail presentation materials to: ____________________

__ Call again at a future date (schedule it in your calendar)
Askfor: ____________________

__ Not a viable dealer for you (Why?)

Teleresearch Worksheet: Institutions/Other Venues

****** Remember -- ANY academic exhibition you can get your work into is an excellent advancement for your career ******

Date of Contact: ___________

Source of Listing: ________
Referred by: _____________

Name of Venue: ______________________________
Affiliation: ______________________________
Address: ______________________________
____
City: ______________________________

Goal of this call:
__ Piece in group show
__ Solo Show
__ Acquire for collection

State: ____________ Zip: _______ Country: ______________________
Telephone: ________________________ Facsimile: ______________________

Director: ________________________ Curator: ______________________
Spoke with: ________________________ Position/Title: ______________________

Venue Hours: ____

What types of art are exhibited in this venue? ______________________________

What is the focus of the venue? ______________________________

How large is the space? Wall footage: ________ Ceiling Height: ___________

Do they show contemporary or traditional artists? __ Contemporary __ Traditional

What type of artists do they show? __ Local __ Regional __ International

What artists are currently in their collection? ______________________________
____

At this point, ask yourself "is my work appropriate for this space?" __ Yes __ No

If "Yes," continue the conversation.
If "No," ask for a referral to another venue.

What are their presentation policies? ______________________________
____
____

To whom should the materials be directed? ________________________________

Remember; if the venue is within driving range of your studio, deliver the presentation materials in person.

How long has this venue been in existence? ________________________________

Do they hold an annual fund raising auction? __ Yes __ No

Will they accept donations from artists for the venue's collection? __ Yes __ No

What is their policy for donations to the venue? ________________________________

____

How often do they change their exhibitions? ________________________________

What were some of their past shows? ________________________________

____

____

____

Who/what/when are their upcoming events? ________________________________

____

____

____

What are the customary promotions done with each show?

__ invitations	__ press releases	__ trade advertisements
__ receptions	__ catalogs	__ tear sheets
__ brochures	__ fliers	__ posters
__ literature	__ other ________________	

Referred by this venue to: ________________________________

____

Next Step: __ Appointment to present to: ________________________________

Date: ____________ Time: ______ Location: ________

__ Mail presentation materials to: ________________________________

__ Call again at a future date (schedule it in your calendar)

Askfor: ________________________________

__ Not a viable venue for you. (Why?)

PRESENTING YOUR WORK

At this point in your career planning, you will begin to come in contact with new people within the art community. Take a moment to tune up your "art etiquette" skills. These guidelines are applicable whenever you contact another person for the purpose of achieving your career goals. Remember, first impressions occur within the first five seconds of one person meeting another.

Art Etiquette to Prevent Art Burn

This is a poignant saying, worth its weight in gold. In few other places within your career plan is the importance of social and "political" propriety ever more important than when you step out to present yourself to the art world. Your reputation, and potentially the reputations of those who may choose to support you, are on the line. A lack of "art etiquette" may result in "art burn," the avoidable diminishment of your success resulting from poorly chosen actions.

Are You the Best Person to Make the Presentation?

Many artists become intimately attached to their work and, more often than not, will take criticisms made about the work very personally. They may not be able to keep their presentation objectives clearly in mind. If this sounds like you, consider selecting a representative to present your work for you. This should be someone who is a member of the art community and knowledgeable about art. This detaches the presenter from the art work, freeing them to focus on the true tasks at hand. However, if the opportunity to present your work arises and you are there, by all means, do not hesitate to do it yourself.

One artist I work with has a very heavy accent and a moderate command of the English language. This often makes it very difficult for him to present his work here in the United States. In this case, selecting a representative to present his work has been very successful.

Time Is Money

The person you are presenting to is a business person whose time is valuable. Be respectful of that. Make an appointment ahead of time. Be prompt to your appointment. Come prepared to give your prepared presentation, limiting it to no more than 15 minutes. Use only those materials designated as your "presentation package." (We will discuss the details of presenting later in this chapter.)

Turn Negatives into Potential Positives

Should you receive a negative response while presenting your work, do not whine, complain or act brashly. Realize that even though you have not received the answer you are looking for, you are still being evaluated by the person. No matter how the negative was thrust upon you, turn that negative into a positive. Let the individual know you respect his or her opinion and then ask whether there is another person he or she may suggest that you contact. Turn every appointment into an information gathering expedition. The person will see that you are professional and serious about your career. Who knows -- you may be referred to the person who will give you your big break.

Act As the Professional You Want to Be

Never be pushy. You will be quickly snubbed by being pushy or brash. In presenting your work, you are looking for someone to invest their time, money, and reputation in the idea that your works are of great importance to their collectors and the art world. You want to convince this person that a venture with you will be a wise and prosperous decision. Why then, would this person wish to risk getting involved with someone who has questionable reliability and is a pain in the neck?

Plan Your Moves Before You Make Them

Planning your moves is very important in building a career. Always formulate a strategy before making any moves. Remember, Rome was not built in a day, and neither will your career be. The best approach in planning your career is to make step-by-step progressions toward your goal -- namely, build your biography with academic exhibitions. Begin with local institutions, progress to regional institutions, then when you are ready and only when you are ready, present to the national academic institutions. If you are an artist approaching the very commercial markets, you will still benefit by growing step-by-step within your venues. Make sure you are able to deliver on your obligations.

Don't Be the Party Wallflower

Social occasions, including receptions on opening nights, are opportunities for you to network and meet the important people of your art community. Standing in the corner will not help you achieve your goals. No matter how shy or limited you are in public, it's time to step out and meet the people.

"Thank You" Is Always Appropriate

Remember to extend a word of thanks to those with whom you come in contact. This may occur when you first greet your invited guests at your opening night event. "Thank you for coming. I hope you enjoy our exhibition." Those whom you view as important people for building your career, i.e., museum curators, dealers, art writers, etc., should be sent a brief thank-you note. Check the registered guest book from your opening. And last, to those important people whom you invited but did not attend, send a catalog, brochure or other material with a personal note. Extend another invitation for them to see your exhibition.

Maintain Your Professional Ethics

Under no circumstance should you ever go around your representation to a collector directly to sell a work in the attempt to save paying a commission. Word of this activity will quickly circulate within the community, and cost you not only your current representation but also any potential of future representation.

Avoid Competing with Your Representation

Handle your independent efforts for promotion and representation diplomatically. Avoid competing with the people who are working on your behalf. For example, if you find yourself in contact with a collector who learned of your work through your gallery, join your gallery into the discussions. Should this collector decide to purchase a work, make sure to keep price integrity with your gallery's offering. Uphold your commission obligations.

Uphold Your Commitments

Be sure to always uphold any obligation you commit yourself to. If you do not believe that you will be able to follow through, do not commit. This is especially important when considering your ability to provide an adequate supply of art works for a gallery. If you can't supply what is needed, let them know. Work to find other options, such as publishing, to fill the need.

Never Present Your Works Unsolicited

It is a common occurrence to see artists driving their works from gallery to gallery with the intent of presenting unsolicited and unprepared. When artists lay out many of their pieces in the gallery this distracts the gallery's clientele from the works that are on actual display. The dealers do not appreciate this, as the artist is taking up their time and interfering with their efforts to earn revenues. This is not the impression you wish to elicit from the dealer.

Before You Begin Presenting...

Before you actually make your presentation, there are a few rules to keep in mind.

1. Do not show your work to a prospective venue unless your materials are in perfect order. Before you go to your appointment or mail your package, make sure all the materials you need are present and accounted for.

2. Always respond in a timely manner. If you have solicited a prospective venue by telephone or in person, it is your duty to make sure everything you have offered to provide to the venue is where it is supposed to be and on time.

3. Keep an open mind to all the possible options. You may be presenting your work with one goal in mind, but the venue may perceive your work in another way on the basis of their needs. Be open to what they have to offer, even if it varies from your original idea.

4. Always be prepared to leave printed materials behind. As you have learned earlier, always have a complete presentation package available for your prospects. It is best to leave something behind for them to be reminded of you.

5. Keep the ball rolling. Once you have made the first contact, keep on top of what is happening. Never let a "hot lead" cool off. A good salesperson knows that once a good lead leaves your grasp, you may never get a second chance.

Presenting in Person

The preferred way to present your work is in person, especially when the venue is within traveling distance from your studio. Request to speak with the person whom you have determined to be the decision maker. If you get to speak to that person or an assistant, arrange for an appointment to present your work. You may have to be persistent to get the appointment. Express your awareness of the venue and how your work relates to its focus and goals. This will help break down some of the barriers.

On Someone Else's Turf

When you present your work on someone else's "turf," certain ground rules apply. Remember, galleries, museums, and universities are businesses, and the people who run them work on a tight schedule. Be considerate of their time. Keep your presentation brief and concise. Unless the person you meet with wishes to continue further, a well-rehearsed presentation should last no longer than fifteen minutes. Second, the materials you bring should be easy to handle. Include your presentation package, and if you wish to bring an actual piece or two, they should be conservative in size, easily carried under one arm. You do not want to look as if you are dragging in the whole farm.

How do you give the presentation? When the person you are meeting greets you, be sure to stand and extend your hand. Thank them at the onset for giving you the opportunity to show them your work.

To avoid any misunderstandings and to keep the appointment on track, clearly establish your intentions at the beginning. For the gallery or dealer, let the person know you are searching for representation in their area. For a museum or other academic institution, state your desire to be included in an upcoming group show, solo show, or in their collection, etc. Your goal will obviously be dictated by the type of venue you are approaching. Part of the purpose of any presentation is to solicit objective opinions of your art.

Next, work briefly through your presentation materials. If you have a catalog or brochure, let them know they are welcome to keep it for their reference. They will receive the first impression of your work from this visual presentation. Mention which pieces are available for exhibition, sale, or loan, whichever is appropriate.

To back up your catalog or brochure images, which are most likely black and white, present the three color prints. The prints show the work in full color to give an idea of how the art appears in a true setting. Give them the opportunity to really take a good look at the pictures. Follow the color pictures with the two black-and-white prints; this shows that you are prepared. The person more often than not will be impressed with your readiness for press by having produced good quality black-and-white prints. The final "presentation" step is to present the full compliment of color slides that match the catalog. Even if you have a full color catalog, you may still wish to present your three color photos and two black-and-whites as well. The richness and impact these prints provide is very important to your presentation.

As you are presenting, give the person time to absorb each piece of information. Be sure not to throw the materials at them. Allow them the chance to get the full impact of your work. Discuss positive points about your work as you present. Mention exhibitions where your work was well received. Do not hesitate to ask questions or solicit recommendations as to where interest in your work may be received.

Close your meeting with a specific request: "I would like you to represent my work." Allow the person a moment to respond. Do not say anything until he or she has had a chance to respond. Be open to what is said and, by all means, do not back the person into a corner by attacking with your question. If you receive a favorable response, you are on your way. If you receive a negative response, ask whether they have any suggestions as to how you may work together, even on a trial basis. Be prepared with a variety of well-thought-out alternatives before you enter into your meeting. Make yourself attractive to that person by being a "low risk" proposition. Keep an open mind and always think of how you could take advantage of this opportunity.

One artist I work with was very successful in a recent presentation by showing a dealer how he, the artist, would be able to bring along new collectors to the gallery. These were people who had purchased his works in the past and were interested in new works, as well as those of other artists. If you have a mailing list of potential contacts for the dealer to work with, you can expand the dealers base in exchange for expanding yours. If you know that one of their collectors has already purchased your work, let them know that.

Remember, even the very best preparation and presentations may result in a "No" response. Many times you will find that, although people like your work, they may not have anything to offer you because of a backlog of prior commitments. It may also be that your work does not truly fit with their focus. Never allow this to discourage you. Again, always ask for a referral as to where they feel you may be able to go next. If they showed interest in your work, put them on your regular mailing list, sending press information, invitations and the like to them as you progress at other events. This will keep you on the forefront of their thoughts. Never allow yourself to be guilty of the phrase "out of sight -- out of mind." Qualify your galleries so you do not waste time.

Always graciously close the meeting with a next step statement, such as "I will call you on Thursday," if that is what they have suggested or, in respect to a referral, "I will call Mr. Hansen this afternoon." No matter which way the personal presentation ends, always send a brief thank-you note for their time. It shows appreciation as well as professionalism. This may go a long way when there becomes space available in a group show or another opportunity arises for which your work may be suitable.

On Your Own Turf

Presenting in person and on your own "turf" is ideal if you have a studio that can comfortably display your work. There are key rules to follow in this type of personal presentation also.

When you schedule an appointment at your own studio, plan to spend at least half an hour and hopefully more with your guest. Give the same type of presentation you would in his or her own venue, except this time you will be able to present a number of the pieces in person. Plan to display in your studio many of the pieces shown in your presentation materials. Put aside pieces that are not related to your presentation to avoid confusing your guest.

A prime example of losing an opportunity by over-presenting your work is an artist I mentioned earlier. He had just returned from presenting his work in New York and was particularly discouraged by the response from one of the more prestigious galleries there; the director, a famous and respected figure in the art community, had recommended that he go home and take up a new profession. After looking at the work he had chosen to present, I could see the director's point. Confronted with thirty years' worth of the artist's best pieces, the director had every reason to be confused.

At the artist's request, I went to his studio to see his current work, which was mature, developed, and quite strong. I felt certain that had he shown that work and that work only in New York, the response would have been a respectable one, even if it didn't include an offer for an exhibition. Once again, we were back to the common question of where and how he might find a market for his art. I contacted an associate at a gallery in Los Angeles and had the artist send properly labeled slides, photographs, and support materials that focused exclusively on the more recent pieces. The director was impressed and agreed to book a show, although he wanted to see the work firsthand.

Although he had a large selection of his early work hung throughout the house, this artist was fortunate enough to have a separate studio where most of his current work was displayed. Having already discussed the reason for the New York gallery's negative response, I emphasized how vital it was that he show only the work that the director had viewed in the presentation package. This was not the time to distract the director with the grand tour of his life's work.

The day after the director visited the studio, he called to say that he would have to decline the show. The artist had chosen to give the full tour, leaving the director more confused than impressed, and that was the end of another great opportunity for that artist.

Presenting Through the Mail

Presenting your work through the mail is acceptable for venues outside reasonable traveling distance from your studio. You do, however, lose some of the impact you can elicit by presenting in person. Use your presentation materials to begin the relationship. Continue to build the relationship through frequent follow-up calls to communicate on the progress of scheduling an exhibition or obtaining representation. If your contact person feels comfortable with you, they will be more apt to do good things for you and to refer you to others in their area. At some point, you may consider making a trip to meet your representative in person at their venue.

Make it a rule to verify the legitimacy and interest of any venue before mailing your presentation materials. Never send any materials to an unsolicited venue. These packages are expensive and if you want them returned, avoid sending unsolicited materials as they may not reach the person for whom they were intended nor be returned to you.

In your teleresearch phone call, ask what their policy is for receiving an artist's presentation package. Ask for the name of the person who reviews such materials, and address the package accordingly. The qualification process you undertake, as directed in the previous chapter, will enhance your chances of having your work reviewed. If you have a personal contact at the venue who knows the reviewer, by all means ask permission to use that name when you approach the venue.

Keep a Log of Your Presentations

Presentation packages are somewhat expensive to create when you consider the costs of reproducing photos, slides and catalogs. It is important for you to keep a current record of each venue and person who has possession of your materials. This will help ensure that you keep in touch with these people as you may have to request that the materials be returned. Again, you may opt to have them keep your catalog or other printed materials. A worksheet has been provided for this purpose.

Follow Up After Presentation

Check back by phone with the people you contacted by mail within four days after their receipt of your materials. Ask whether they have had a chance to review your work and whether you may possibly set up an appointment to meet in person. Whether the response was a positive or negative one, always send a note thanking them for taking the time to review your work.

Presentation Tracking Worksheet

Once you have organized and completed your presentation packages, you are ready to begin qualifying and presenting your work to targeted venues. Use this worksheet to track the sequence of steps within each presentation.

Contact Venue: *Sonova Gallery*

✓ Teleresearch call. Initial introduction of artist to the qualified venue.

✓ Personally present or mail the complete presentation package including a personalized cover letter reflecting the key points discussed in the initial conversation.

✓ Within at least four days of the presentation, call the package recipient to make sure the package was received (if mailed) and/or to determine if they have had the opportunity to review your materials.

✓ Send the appropriate follow-up letter as prescribed in the chapter "Written Communications."

✓ Continue to follow-up with the venue, calling and sending correspondence until a final answer either positive or negative is received. Remember, however, not to be overly pushy or "grind" the venue. Simply stay in regular contact.

✓ If a commitment was made, send a confirmation letter detailing all the terms of the agreement which was reached for exhibition, representation or other. You may decide to allow this venue to keep the presentation package for their sales and promotional purposes or you may allow the venue to keep the catalog and return the other materials for future presentation.

__ Send a thank-you note for their time and efforts in reviewing your work. You may request your materials be returned, offering to let the venue keep your catalog for future reference.

__ If a certain amount of interest was expressed in your work but no commitment was made at this time, place this venue on your mailing list. Send regular notes, articles, invitations or the like to your contact to keep them abreast of the progress your career is making. Above all else, actively work your mailing list.

Presentation Log Worksheet

[✓] Returned **[✓] Checked Out**

Date of Presentation: *02 / 20 / 93*
To Whom: *Catherine Kingston* Telephone: *(213) 555-8910*
Location: *The Contemporary Museum* G / M / I / Other
Presentation: ✓ In Person __ By a Rep __ Via Mail __ Other ______
Materials Used: ✓ Standard Package ✓ Other Requested keep catalog for their library
Date Return Requested: *03 / 01 / 93*
Date Materials Returned: *Kept - Show Pending*

[__] Returned **[✓] Checked Out**

Date of Presentation: *02 / 25 / 93*
To Whom: *Mathew Hillsing* Telephone: *(212) 555-0046*
Location: *Sonova Gallery* G / M / I / Other
Presentation: __ In Person __ By a Rep ✓ Via Mail __ Other ______
Materials Used: ✓ Standard Package __ Other ______
Date Return Requested: *03 / 01 / 93*
Date Materials Returned: *03 / 15 / 93*

[__] Returned **[__] Checked Out**

Date of Presentation: ______
To Whom: ______ Telephone: ______
Location: ______ G / M / I / Other
Presentation: __ In Person __ By a Rep __ Via Mail __ Other ______
Materials Used: __ Standard Package __ Other ______
Date Return Requested: ______
Date Materials Returned: ______

[__] Returned **[__] Checked Out**

Date of Presentation: ______
To Whom: ______ Telephone: ______
Location: ______ G / M / I / Other
Presentation: __ In Person __ By a Rep __ Via Mail __ Other ______
Materials Used: __ Standard Package __ Other ______
Date Return Requested: ______
Date Materials Returned: ______

WRITTEN COMMUNICATIONS

The written word can provide great strength to your presentation. It is important for you to be aware of how to write a professional letter properly. There are a number of good books written on the subject, providing the grammatical and structural guidelines appropriate for such communication. Invest a few dollars in one of these books to keep at your desk for reference. A number of specific examples of artist's letters are included in this book.

This chapter highlights writing professional cover letters, follow-up letters, thank-you notes and resumes -- the key writing you will need to undertake in your marketing plan. Writing for the purposes of promotion, such as press releases, will be covered in the chapter "Promotions."

Stationery

The writing papers used in a presentation are simple, clean, and professional. You can find the guidelines for formatting letterhead in any business writing book but, in summary, your name, complete address, telephone number and facsimile number, if available, are centered at the top of the letter. Avoid using flamboyant logos or type that only serve to clutter the presentation. It may seem boring, but it is appropriate.

Use a good quality paper. Avoid onion skin, erasable typing paper, and the like. A 20-pound bond is quite effective. White or soft cream papers are the most appropriate; other colors, again, can become too slick. A standard size of 8-1/2" x 11" is proper. Refrain from using personal size paper, which is smaller than the overall size of the presentation package.

The mailing envelope for a presentation package should be a size larger than the presentation itself to avoid bending the photographs and catalog. Use an envelope that is slightly padded to protect the package. Envelopes for follow-up letters not accompanied by materials should match the size, color, and type of the writing paper the letter was printed on.

Check Your Spelling

Once you have gone to the effort to create a good letter, it is imperative that the spelling and grammar are proof read. If you do not feel confident in your abilities to do this, have someone else proof it for you. Few things are less professional than mailing a letter with typos and misspellings. This added step will save you from embarrassment.

Confirm that you are using the proper spelling of the recipient's name, title and business before sending the letter. If you are unsure, make another call to confirm that all is correct. When it is right, people tend not to notice, but when it is wrong, it sticks out like a sore thumb.

Fonts and Printing

Given today's age of computers, I strongly suggest that all letters be printed on some type of laser printer. The quality of the print and the presentation value it provides is superior to dot matrix printers or typewriters. If you do not have a laser printer of your own, you can go to almost any copy center or word processing service to rent time on their computers. It is not expensive, but it goes a long way in the presentation. If you feel you can not afford a service such as this, at least use a typewriter. Again, do not hand write your letters except for possibly thank-you cards or notes.

Select a font that is contemporary, clean, and easy to read. As you avoided using creative logos on the letterhead, refrain from using stylized fonts that may be difficult to read. Your goal is to communicate clearly.

Length of a Letter

The very best letters are short and to the point. Begin with a complimentary or referral opening statement, something to attract interest. Then move right into the point of your letter once the opening has laid the introductory groundwork. Refrain from using flowery language and overly exhaustive sentences. One artist I work with writes well, but each sentence is at least a paragraph in length. This should be avoided.

Standardizing Your Letter Library

It is important for you to create your own library of commonly used letters, including standard cover letters for each venue type, follow-up letters and thank-you notes. When the time comes to mail to a prospective venue, select the letter that is most appropriate for the situation. Personalize the addressing of the letter and make the necessary changes in the text of the letter. You will spend less time coordinating packages once you have established your own library.

Please be sure to understand that I do not mean for you to photocopy a slew of standard, non-directed letters starting with "Dear Venue." Each letter must be personalized to the recipient of the letter. The library is a standardization of the body of the text or the "meat" of the letter.

Keep Files of All Communications

As with the archive of all your presentation materials, it is important for you to keep a record of all communications coming in and going out of your studio. Each time you send a letter, make a copy of it for yourself. Create a filing system so that you can track your letters out and the responses you receive back. One of the most effective methods is to make a file for each venue you are soliciting, place all communications and information into that file, and then store each in alphabetical order in a convenient filing drawer. This will make the file quickly accessible any time you are either writing to or talking with that venue. Organization of your office communications is one of the keys to success.

Format of the Page

The format of a business letter is quite simple, as shown on the following page. Keep to this format unless you find another in your reference that is more suited to your writing style.

Feedback About Your Letter-Writing Techniques

Writing a good business letter is a developed skill for most people. It requires practice and observation. Keep track of the letters that elicit the strongest responses from the recipients. If you have created an usually strong letter, put it in your library and use it again.

Mr./Mrs./Ms. Your Name
Your Street Address
Your City, State Zip Code
Telephone - Facsimile

Current Date

Mr./Mrs./Ms. Recipient Name
Recipient Business Name
Recipient Street Address
Recipient City, State Zip Code

Dear Mr./Mrs./Ms. Recipient Last Name: (Or Dear First Name: if you are on a first-name basis)

(Body of letter)

Sincerely,

Your Full Name (excluding Mr./Mrs./Ms. salutation)

- -

Ms. Lanna Langtree
1556 South Watkins Drive
Los Angeles, CA 90046
(213) 555-1212

January 1, 1993

Mr. Mathew Hillsing
Sonova Gallery
408 Greene Street
New York, NY 10012

Dear Mr. Hillsing:

(Body of letter)

Sincerely,

Lanna Langtree

Cover Letters

For our purposes, the presentation cover letter is designed to reintroduce you and your art to the prospective venue. This letter is designed to arrive to the venue after an initial solicitation and introduction call has been made. Remember never to send any of your materials out unsolicited. Whenever you write any letter for presentation, keep the recipient's needs in mind, focusing your presentation to fulfill their needs.

The opening paragraph of your letter is designed to remind the recipient of your earlier phone call and to introduce the idea that you are presenting quality works for review. If you were referred to this person by someone, such as a collector, who may be important to the venue, state this in the opening.

Next, make a specific statement about your work in the next paragraph. Be brief and to the point, noting the strengths of your art and your exhibition experience to this point. Make a statement that draws a direct correlation between your art and the goals and focus of the venue. This should make the recipient more comfortable with the idea of accepting your art into their venue.

The final paragraph is a statement to action. What is it that you would like this person to do? Be clear about your intention. Plan what steps need to be taken and ask for the first step. This may be, for example, to meet with the recipient in person at his or her location or to have the recipient visit your studio. As the saying goes, if you do not ask, you will not receive.

You may find other outlines for your cover letters that suit your style and personality more closely. The guidelines and examples are those with which I have found continued success, the focus of each being derived from the initial telephone contact. Use what works for you. The following letters are examples of how a cover letter for your presentation package may be written. Use the worksheet provided to create two to three presentation cover letters for your library.

Cover Letter with Personal Referral - For the Gallery

Ms. Michelle Talvison
1556 South Watkins Drive
Los Angeles, CA 90046
(213) 555-1212

January 1, 1993

Mr. Mathew Hillsing
Sonova Gallery
408 Greene Street
New York, NY 10012

Dear Mathew:

It was a pleasure speaking with you this morning. As I mentioned, one of your collectors, Carol Carlotel, suggested I contact you. After personally reviewing my work, she thought the style, strength and media in my work would be interesting to you and very saleable through your gallery.

My work has been widely exhibited on the west coast and pacific rim, including the Mockteller Museum in San Francisco; the Alternative Museum in Los Angeles and the Modern Museum in San Diego. A number of your collectors have purchased my work over the past few years and have expressed continued interest in acquiring new pieces. They each have expressed their attraction to my unique use of color and found objects which lure the viewer into the painting.

Mathew, I have enclosed presentation materials for your review, including a catalog from my current show at the Blumschmelt Gallery. I will call you again next week to discuss the possibility of your gallery representing my work.

Sincerely,

Michelle Talvison

Encl. Presentation Materials

Cover Letter with Personal Referral - For the Museum

Ms. Michelle Talvison
1556 South Watkins Drive
Los Angeles, CA 90046
(213) 555-1212

January 1, 1993

Ms. Catherine Kingston
Curator
The Contemporary Museum
5504 Broad St.
Los Angeles, CA 90046

Dear Ms. Kingston:

It was a pleasure speaking with you this morning. As I mentioned, Robert Gaffey, a board member of your museum, suggested I contact you. After personally visiting my exhibition at the Rothkeller Institute, he felt the style, media and subject matter of my work ties directly into the focus of your museum.

My work has been widely exhibited on the west coast and pacific rim, including the Mockteller Museum in San Francisco; the Alternative Museum in Los Angeles and the Modern Museum in San Diego. The intensity of my paintings has been compared to that of Richter, Michaels and Bellington. Each piece addresses issues confronting society today.

Catherine, I have enclosed presentation materials for your review, including a catalog from my current show at the Blumschmelt Gallery. I will call you again next week to discuss your response to my work and your interest in the possibility of exhibition.

Sincerely,

Michelle Talvison

Encl. Presentation Materials

Cover Letter without Personal Referral - For the Gallery

Ms. Kelly Bryson
3502 Brookshire Glen
Los Angeles, CA 90046
(213) 555-1236

January 1, 1993

Mr. Mathew Hillsing
Sonova Gallery
408 Greene Street
New York, NY 10012

Dear Mathew:

It was a pleasure speaking with you this morning. As I mentioned, I have recently seen your advertisements in various national art magazines and have been impressed with the quality of work you represent. I am interested in exposure of my work on the east coast and believe the style, strength and media of my art may be interesting to you and very saleable through your gallery.

My strong use of color with symbolism is reminiscent of Resnick and Newman. I am serious about my career and am interested in working with a dealer such as yourself to accomplish not only my goals but help you to accomplish yours.

Mathew, I have enclosed presentation materials for your review. I will call you again next week to discuss the possibility of your gallery representing my work.

Sincerely,

Kelly Bryson

Encl. Presentation Materials

** ***This letter is an example of how an entry level artist presenting their work for the first time can create credibility without exposing their inexperience.***

Cover Letter without Personal Referral - For the Museum

Ms. Michelle Talvison
1556 South Watkins Drive
Los Angeles, CA 90046
(213) 555-1212

January 1, 1993

Ms. Catherine Kingston
Curator
The Contemporary Museum
5504 Broad St.
Los Angeles, CA 90046

Dear Ms. Kingston:

It was a pleasure speaking with you this morning. As I mentioned, I recently attended the opening of your Brockmeyer Retrospective where I observed that the style, media and subject matter of my work ties directly into the focus of your museum.

My work has been widely exhibited on the west coast and pacific rim, including the Mockteller Museum in San Francisco; the Alternative Museum in Los Angeles and the Modern Museum in San Diego. The intensity of my paintings has been compared to that of Richter, Michaels and Bellington. Each piece addresses issues confronting society today.

Catherine, I have enclosed presentation materials for your review, including a catalog from my current show at the Blumschmelt Gallery. I will call you again next week to discuss your response to my work and your interest in the possibility of exhibition.

Sincerely,

Michelle Talvison

Encl. Presentation Materials

Presentation Cover Letter Worksheet

(Date) *January 1, 1993*

(Name) *Mathew Hillsing*
(Title) *Director*
(Venue) *Sonova Gallery*
(Address) *408 Greene St.*
(City) *New York* **(State)** *NY* **(Zip)** *10012*

Dear: *Mathew*

Opening Paragraph:

(Remind Phone Call) *It was a pleasure speaking with you this morning. As I mentioned, one of your collectors, Carol Carlotel, suggested I contact you.*

(Presenting Your Art) *After personally reviewing my work, she thought the style, strength and media in my work would be interesting to you and very saleable through your gallery.*

Second Paragraph:

(Strength of Your Art) *My work has been widely exhibited on the west coast and pacific rim, including the Mockteller (SF), Alternative Museum (LA) and Modern Museum (SD).*

(Tie-in Statement) *A number of your collectors have purchased my work over the past few years and have expressed continued interest in acquiring new pieces. They have expressed their attraction to my unique use of color and found objects which lure the viewer into the painting.*

Closing Paragraph:

(Call to Action) *I have enclosed presentation materials for your review, including a catalog from my current show at the Blumschmelt Gallery.*

(Your Follow-up Step) *I will call you again next week to discuss the possibility of your gallery representing my work.*

Sincerely,

(Your Name) *Michelle Talvison*

Follow-up Letters

The purpose of a follow-up letter is to keep the communication lines open and your prospect moving positively from one step to the next. The nature of this letter will be determined by the response or lack of response you have received from your initial contacts with the prospective venue.

In at least four days after sending or presenting your materials, make a follow-up call. Your presence on the phone will bring you to the forefront of the person's thought. You will be able to assess his or her impressions of your work. This is a test reading as the recipient may not have had a chance to review your work thoroughly, but your interaction with this person has made an impression.

When you have mailed the presentation, this follow up call can be used to ensure that your package was received by the proper person. If not received, it is worth your while to trace it down. Many artists will go to the additional expense of using an express mail service just for their ability to track the package.

Once your call is complete, follow it up with a brief letter. The following three basic types of standardized follow up letters should be created for your library.

1: Soliciting a Response

This type of letter is designed to solicit a response in cases in which the package has been received but not yet reviewed. This letter will restate the second and third paragraphs of your cover letter in a bit more depth. The follow-up letter is again selling your art as something worth the other's time and interest to pursue.

2: The Positive Response Follow-up

This type of letter is designed to "keep the ball rolling." When a positive response is received from the venue, following a personal meeting, for example, it is important to put down in writing the agreements or proposed plans that were discussed. Your letter will restate the substance of the discussion in brief. Close with a statement of what happens next. If you were asked to provide materials or information, enclose them with this letter.

Whenever you are dealing with a venue and commitments have been made to you verbally, it is imperative that you confirm these commitments in writing. You never know when your contact person will move on in his or her career to be replaced by someone else. You need to obtain a binding agreement, signed by both the venue and yourself. There are too many stories to relate of exhibitions lost by the lack of a written commitment.

3: The Negative Response Follow-up

The next type of letter is used following a negative response. As you learned earlier, it is your job to turn a negative response into something positive. Use this letter to gain referrals from the venue. This letter should be a gracious close to your pursuit of this venue, leaving the door open for a future date and for you to obtain names of the people who, in this persons's professional opinion, would be worth your while to contact. Do not grind people who aren't amenable to selling or showing your work in their venue.

Soliciting a Response

Ms. Michelle Talvison
1556 South Watkins Drive
Los Angeles, CA 90046
(213) 555-1212

January 5, 1993

Mr. Mathew Hillsing
Sonova Gallery
408 Greene Street
New York, NY 10012

Dear Mathew:

Thank you for your compliments regarding the promptness of my response to your request for materials. As you will see, I enclosed a catalog from one of my recent exhibitions, the essay of which was written by the noted critic, Linda Brock.

My work has received wide acclaim through numerous exhibitions on the west coast and pacific rim, including the Mockteller Museum in San Francisco; the Alternative Museum in Los Angeles and the Modern Museum in San Diego. A number of your collectors have purchased my work over the past few years and have expressed continued interest in acquiring new pieces. They each have expressed their attraction to my unique use of color and found objects which lure the viewer into the painting. This uniqueness has created a willingness in the collectors to pay an exceptional price for my work.

Mathew, I will call you again next week to talk about the possibility of your gallery representing my work. I look forward to discussing the mutual benefits we can bring to each other.

Sincerely,

Michelle Talvison

Positive Response Follow-up

Ms. Michelle Talvison
1556 South Watkins Drive
Los Angeles, CA 90046
(213) 555-1212

January 5, 1993

Mr. Mathew Hillsing
Sonova Gallery
408 Greene Street
New York, NY 10012

Dear Mathew:

The opportunity you have presented to exhibit my work in your upcoming group exhibition is very exciting. I am confident my work will help further your reputation for exhibiting and selling quality art.

As we discussed, I will consign the pieces ***"The Depth of Conscious"*** and ***"Grand Illusion"*** to your gallery for the length of the show, March 15th through April 12th, 1993. During that time, you will have the exclusive right to represent and sell these works. If the pieces are not sold during that time, you will ship and insure the pieces back to my studio by April 19th. I have enclosed a signed copy of the consignment agreement we reviewed which confirms these arrangements.

Mathew, I am presently arranging for the crating and shipment of these works so that they arrive at your gallery on March 12th as you requested. I will contact you next week with the details regarding jointly producing a group catalog for this exhibition just as I did for my recent solo exhibition.

Sincerely,

Michelle Talvison

Encl. Signed Consignment Agreement

Negative Response Follow-up

Ms. Michelle Talvison
1556 South Watkins Drive
Los Angeles, CA 90046
(213) 555-1212

January 5, 1993

Mr. Mathew Hillsing
Sonova Gallery
408 Greene Street
New York, NY 10012

Dear Mathew:

Thank you for reviewing the presentation of my work. Your suggestion to contact Lou Mac to investigate publishing a mixed media limited edition of the two pieces ***"The Depth of Conscious"*** and ***"Grand Illusion"*** interests me. As a gesture of thanks should an edition be produced, I would like to offer you first choice of a piece for your gallery.

Mathew, if you have any ideas of whom else may be interested in my work, I would greatly appreciate the contact. I will keep in touch and let you know of the progress of my career. I genuinely enjoyed our conversations.

Sincerely,

Michelle Talvison

Follow-up Letter Worksheet
Soliciting a Response

(Date) ____________________

(Name) ________________________
(Title) ________________________
(Venue) ______________________
(Address) ____________________
(City) _________________________ **(State)** ___ **(Zip)** __________

Dear _____________________:

Opening Paragraph:

(Welcome/Remind Phone Call) ____
____

(Prompt to Review Materials) ____

Second Paragraph:

(Restate Strengths of Your Art) ____
____
____
____

(Restate Tie-in Statement) ____
____

Closing Paragraph:

(Call to Action) ____
____
____

(Follow-up Step) ____
____

Sincerely,

(Your Name) ___________________________________

Follow-up Letter Worksheet
Positive Response

(Date) ____________________

(Name) ________________________
(Title) __________________________
(Venue) ________________________
(Address) ______________________
(City) ___________________________ **(State)** ___ **(Zip)** ___________

Dear ______________________:

Opening Paragraph:

(Appreciation Statement) ____
Look forward to ... ____
It was a pleasure ... ____

(Materials Enclosed) ____

Second Paragraph:

(Brief Recap of Discussion) ____
____
____
____

(Agreed-upon Actions) ____
____

Closing Paragraph:

(Next Step(s)) ____
____

(Your Follow-up Step) ____

Sincerely,

(Your Name) ______________________________________

Follow-up Letter Worksheet
Negative Response -- Referral Request

(Date) ____________________

(Name) ____________________
(Title) ____________________
(Venue) ____________________
(Address) ____________________
(City) ____________________ **(State)** ___ **(Zip)** __________

Dear ____________________:

Opening Paragraph:

(Thank-you Statement) ____________________
____

Second Paragraph

(Request for Referrals) ____________________
____
____

Closing Paragraph:

(Welcome Future Contact) ____________________
____

Sincerely,

(Your Name) ____________________

Thank-you Notes

Thank-you notes are appropriate for all occasions. Always remember to extend a word of thanks to those with whom you come in contact. This is appropriate whether the response you receive is positive or negative, especially after personal presentations. Don't go overboard, but be sure to thank those who have taken their time to help you.

Constant Communications

Many artists have found that they can receive rapid success by using a constant communication network with the art community. They are always sending out information in the form of letters, invitations, notes, and the like to keep their collectors and those who are helpful to their career informed of what is happening. Artists who do this are able to generate name recognition in their targeted market and through the press. Never allow dead time to pass during which you are not beating on one door or another with the good news of what is happening with your art.

The Professional Artist's Resume

The artist's resume is a complete synopsis of exhibition experience, grants and awards, professional experience, education, collectors, editorials, and publications. The purpose of the resume is to give the reader a full understanding of your involvement and accomplishments within the art world. The resume will be used to supplement the selected biography within your printed presentation materials.

If you are an artist just starting out, you may not be far enough along to have a complete resume. That is all right. You may choose to use only certain pieces of the full resume, focusing on the purpose for your use of it.

Appearance Is Important

In an earlier chapter, we discussed how to create the first impression of your work using the cover image on your catalog or brochure. The same need for strength in appearance applies to your resume. An artist's resume must be written concisely, with clarity, and printed in an easy-to-read format. The rules regarding paper selection, font styles, laser printing, and proofing we discussed earlier in this chapter apply here as well.

Elements of a Resume

The content of your resume tells a story of your accomplishments within the art world. Therefore, it is important to include information that impresses upon the reader the importance of your art. You must show the reader a record of your experience and documentation of your qualifications.

Biographical Statement

The first element is a brief, biographical statement including your birth date, location, and a synopsis of your development as an artist. This statement is written in the same tone as the academic essay so include references to important artists or professionals with whom you have studied, worked, or been influenced by. All this information should be stated in no more than two brief paragraphs.

Recent Selected Exhibitions

List your exhibitions in chronological order going back from two to five years with the current year listed first. This will demonstrate your current activities as a professional artist. Include all institutional events, gallery showings, juried competitions, or selected important benefit events. Avoid listing restaurant shows and the like that do not necessarily fall under the category of academic events (unless of course, you are pursuing the more commercial marketplace.) If there were important events earlier in your career, by all means, include those in your exhibition listing, but remove the term "recent" from the heading. The biography will demonstrate that your work is out there being seen by the art community and that you are a serious, producing artist.

Format each entry beginning with the year of the event, title of the exhibition, name of the institution or gallery holding the event, and the city, state, and country location of the event. For events occurring in the same year, list the year once and let the format of the page show the remaining entries occurred in the same year. For example:

1993	"A Room with a View" Modern Museum of Art Santa Ana, California, USA	"A Woman of Strength" The Woman's Contemporary Museum Los Angeles, California, USA

Present the information in as academic a fashion as possible. Give the name of a location correctly but make it as academic sounding as possible. One-person shows that did not have a specific title may be referenced as "Your Name." Above all else, be honest with what you say in your biography. You can count on the fact that anyone seriously considering showing your work will check you out thoroughly.

Depending on your preference, you may list solo exhibitions separately from group exhibitions. My preference is to do so if the artist has had a fair number of solo shows. If the artist has had primarily group events, I would group these together. When solo shows are listed separately, use the heading "Selected Solo Exhibitions." In turn, title the group exhibitions "Selected Group Exhibitions." List all solo shows in chronological order before starting the new section for group exhibitions.

Awards, Honors, and Grants

The next element is to show the reader that you have earned various awards, honors or grants; recognition for the importance of your work to the art community. These entries are listed in precisely the same format as an exhibition entry, for example:

1993	"Randall Francis Community Grant" The Randall Francis Foundation Los Angeles, California, USA

List all important honors. This will show the reader your acceptance within the art world and recognition of the importance of your work. You will be perceived as active and dedicated to your art, an important impression to give to a prospective venue.

Selected Collections

Listing the important collections your work is part of is an important element to your resume. Include personal, corporate, and institutional collections in your resume. If your works are collected by someone who is respected within the art world, your work is perceived to be worthy of the level of importance of these collections. Your work will begin to rise in importance and its value based on the company it keeps.

List the collections by the collection names and not the collectors, unless that is the manner in which they are commonly referred. Avoid referencing family members, unless they are important art collectors. No one will want to see that your work hangs in your parents' home.

Collection entries are formatted with the name of the collection and the city, state, and country of their location. For example, the Brunheiber Collection is located in New York. The entry would read:

> The Brunheiber Collection
> New York, NY, USA

Professional Experience

This element of the resume shows the reader your background above and beyond the exhibitions you have had. The professional experience relates to those things you have done and accomplished as a professional artist, such as, lectures you may have given, teaching you may have provided to artists, participation in artist-in-residence programs, and the like. Do not list things you have done outside the art community unless they are directly tied to your work.

Education

The importance of education has been reflected throughout this book. It is your key to understanding the historical and contemporary influences of the art around you. It will help you to understand your own place within the art world. This information is a part of the early biographical section of the resume and important to also include.

Do not be concerned if your education is limited, although in some cases it can help to have an extensive education. The important thing is that your work is strong. Include what education you do have as well as with whom you have studied.

Publications

It is always impressive to list those catalogs and publications in which your work is shown. Again, you are establishing the importance of your art to the reader. Any magazines, books, news articles, and the like that discussed your work should also be included. This information is listed in a format similar to that you would find in a bibliography for a book report. Remember to always include the author's name.

CARMEN STAVROS

Born: 1953, Scottsdale, Arizona.

Stavros studied Fine Arts at Arizona State University and the Art Institute of Southern California. She also studied with Roger Armestead, Sam Clayburn, George Galliger, Tom Gallant, Robert Wing, and Milford Zin. Stavros has her Bachelors and Masters degrees in Fine Arts. She is known in the southwestern art community for her strong compositions and her vibrant use of color.

RECENT SOLO EXHIBITIONS

1990 "Carmen Stavros"
Harthbrook Museum
Scottsdale, AZ, USA

1991 "Sticks and Stones"
Gavin Smith Gallery
Los Angeles, CA, USA

1991 "A Woman in Motion"
South Bay Gallery
Pasadena, CA, USA

1992 "Stick Figures"
Art in Space Museum
New York, NY, USA

1992 "Glass Houses"
Art in Space Museum
New York, NY, USA

1993 "She Sez"
Cantorland Gallery
Chicago, IL, USA

RECENT GROUP EXHIBITIONS

1990 "Currents"
Time Stop Gallery
Scottsdale, AZ, USA

1990 "Tide Watch"
Southern Artists Museum
Scottsdale, AZ, USA

1991 "Stavros, Smith & Watson"
Southern Artists Museum
Scottsdale, AZ, USA

1991 "Women in Motion"
South Bay Gallery
Pasadena, CA, USA

1992 "Still Life -- After Life"
Art in Space Museum
New York, NY, USA

1992 "Woman Media"
Gavin Smith Gallery
Los Angeles, CA, USA

1992 "Currents"
Time Space Gallery
Laguna Beach, CA, USA

1993 "Sacred Signals"
Grace Main Gallery
New York, NY, USA

AWARDS AND HONORS

1992 "Randall Francis Community Grant"
The Randall Francis Foundation
Los Angeles, CA, USA

1992 Female Artist of the Year
Southern States Artist Guild
Los Angeles, CA, USA

SELECTED COLLECTIONS

State University Fine Arts Museum
Imperial University
English Council of Fine Arts
Cleveland Museum of Contemporary Arts
The Hopkins Estate

PROFESSIONAL EXPERIENCE

1992 "Sculpture with Wood," Lecture Series, California College, Los Angeles, CA.

EDUCATION

1971-74 Bachelor of Fine Art, Arizona State University.
1974-77 Master of Fine Art, Art Institute of Southern California.

PUBLICATIONS

Anderson, Julian. THE STRENGTH OF WOMEN IN ART, Catalog, The Southern States Artist Guild, Oct. 30 - Dec. 9, 1991.

Beckton, William. CARMEN STAVROS - A WOMAN IN MOTION, Catalog, The Southern States Art Guild, Jan. 15 - Feb. 10, 1992.

Feather, Anthony. PUTTING DOWN FOUNDATIONS, Feminist Art World, Vol 3, No 6, December, 1992, p 35.

Stavros, Carmen. STICKS AND STONES, Catalog, Gavin Smith Gallery, Feb. 15 - Mar. 1, 1991.

Thomas, Anthony. GLASS HOUSES, Arts Institutional, Vol 6, No 2, February, 1992.

Wiggins, Daniel. CURRENTS, Catalog, Time Space Gallery, Aug. 15 - Sep. 1, 1992.

CAREER PLAN

Resume Writing Worksheet

(Your Name) ____

(Year of Birth) ____________________

(City, State, Country of Birth) ______________________________

Biography:

Recent Selected Solo Exhibitions:

(Year) ____________ (Exhibition Title) ________________________
(Location) ________________________
(City, State, Cntry) ________________________

(Year) ____________ (Exhibition Title) ________________________
If Different (Location) ________________________
(City, State, Cntry) ________________________

(Year) ____________ (Exhibition Title) ________________________
If Different (Location) ________________________
(City, State, Cntry) ________________________

(Year) ____________ (Exhibition Title) ________________________
If Different (Location) ________________________
(City, State, Cntry) ________________________

(Year) ____________ (Exhibition Title) ________________________
If Different (Location) ________________________
(City, State, Cntry) ________________________

(Year) ____________ (Exhibition Title) ________________________
If Different (Location) ________________________
(City, State, Cntry) ________________________

(Year) ____________ (Exhibition Title) ________________________
If Different (Location) ________________________
(City, State, Cntry) ________________________

(Year) ____________ (Exhibition Title) ________________________
If Different (Location) ________________________
(City, State, Cntry) ________________________

(Year) ____________ (Exhibition Title) ________________________
If Different (Location) ________________________
(City, State, Cntry) ________________________

(Year) ____________ (Exhibition Title) ________________________
If Different (Location) ________________________
(City, State, Cntry) ________________________

Repeat this section as many times as is necessary to complete your listing.

Recent Selected Group Exhibitions:

(Year) ____________ (Exhibition Title) ____________________
(Location) ____________________
(City, State, Cntry) ____________________

(Year) ____________ (Exhibition Title) ____________________
If Different (Location) ____________________
(City, State, Cntry) ____________________

(Year) ____________ (Exhibition Title) ____________________
If Different (Location) ____________________
(City, State, Cntry) ____________________

(Year) ____________ (Exhibition Title) ____________________
If Different (Location) ____________________
(City, State, Cntry) ____________________

(Year) ____________ (Exhibition Title) ____________________
If Different (Location) ____________________
(City, State, Cntry) ____________________

(Year) ____________ (Exhibition Title) ____________________
If Different (Location) ____________________
(City, State, Cntry) ____________________

(Year) ____________ (Exhibition Title) ____________________
If Different (Location) ____________________
(City, State, Cntry) ____________________

(Year) ____________ (Exhibition Title) ____________________
If Different (Location) ____________________
(City, State, Cntry) ____________________

(Year) ____________ (Exhibition Title) ____________________
If Different (Location) ____________________
(City, State, Cntry) ____________________

(Year) ____________ (Exhibition Title) ____________________
If Different (Location) ____________________
(City, State, Cntry) ____________________

Repeat this section as many times as is necessary to complete your listing.

Awards, Honors, and Grants:

(Year) ____________ (Title) ____________________
(Presented By) ____________________
(City, State, Cntry) ____________________

(Year) ____________ (Title) ____________________
If Different (Presented By) ____________________
(City, State, Cntry) ____________________

(Year) ____________ (Title) ____________________
If Different (Presented By) ____________________
(City, State, Cntry) ____________________

(Year) ____________ (Title) ____________________
If Different (Presented By) ____________________
(City, State, Cntry) ____________________

(Year) ____________ (Title) ____________________
If Different (Presented By) ____________________
(City, State, Cntry) ____________________

Selected Collections:

(Name of Collection) ____________________
(City, State, Cntry) ____________________

(Name of Collection) ____________________
(City, State, Cntry) ____________________

(Name of Collection) ____________________
(City, State, Cntry) ____________________

(Name of Collection) ____________________
(City, State, Cntry) ____________________

(Name of Collection) ____________________
(City, State, Cntry) ____________________

(Name of Collection) ____________________
(City, State, Cntry) ____________________

Repeat this section as many times as is necessary to complete your listing.

Professional Experience:

____

____

____

____

Education:

(Year) __________ (Degree) _______________
(Institution) _______________
(City, State, Cntry) _______________

(Year) __________ (Degree) _______________
(Institution) _______________
(City, State, Cntry) _______________

(Year) __________ (Degree) _______________
(Institution) _______________
(City, State, Cntry) _______________

Publications:

(Author) ____________ (Title) ____________________
(Sponsor) ____________ (Type of Publication) ______________
(Date/Year) ____________

(Author) ____________ (Title) ____________________
(Sponsor) ____________ (Type of Publication) ______________
(Date/Year) ____________

(Author) ____________ (Title) ____________________
(Sponsor) ____________ (Type of Publication) ______________
(Date/Year) ____________

(Author) ____________ (Title) ____________________
(Sponsor) ____________ (Type of Publication) ______________
(Date/Year) ____________

WORKING WITH THE VENUE
THE BUSINESS OF BEING AN ARTIST

Getting right down to it, a career as a professional artist entails being aware of and participating in various business practices established for your protection and that of the venue or representative. These practices include the reading and signing of contractual agreements, the documentation of art from venue to venue, and the tracking of the fulfillment of obligations by yourself and your venue. In this chapter, numerous standard forms and documents are provided for your use. Take the time to become familiar with each form, what it means, when to use it, and how it will be of benefit to you.

Read Before You Sign

Whenever you are approached with a contractual agreement, read it in its entirety before you sign. Be sure to know the details of what you are obligating yourself to and what compensation you will be receiving for your efforts. It is my recommendation to have an attorney review all contracts submitted to you before signing. Prepare copies of your own standard agreements, such as those provided in this book, and confirm with your attorney that you are properly covered should you use these documents in the course of your business. Keep in mind that attorneys bill for their time. Be organized with your presentation of documents and know what your attorney will charge for this service ahead of time. Don't allow yourself to be surprised with a large attorney bill simply because you didn't ask. Avoid "handshake agreements."

What Is Expected of You

Once you have obtained a representative, an exhibition, or funding, be sure you understand your obligations. Make a time line in your calendar of when obligations are due, planning adequate lead time to complete what is needed. Be prepared to take on the responsibilities for framing your works, shipping your works, ensuring the works against damage during that shipment, and so on. These are the details that will erode your profit margin if not addressed at the time you make your agreement. Each venue has different business practices and needs. It is your responsibility to know those practices ahead of time as part of your venue qualifying efforts. Do not allow yourself to be surprised.

What You Should Expect from Your Venue

When you obtain representation, the costs of shipping the works to the gallery for exhibition are often not covered by the gallery. The return shipment of consigned pieces, however, is usually taken care of by the gallery. Clarify all of these arrangements ahead of time. The issue of insuring the works during shipment is something to be negotiated between you and the dealer at the onset.

Galleries generally pay for the promotion of the exhibition, including invitations, mailings, opening-night parties, press releases, and so on. Remember, however, you may find yourself pitching in where the gallery needs help. Be sure to have all expense reimbursements agreed to and signed before you begin. It is customary for all parties who have expended funds for the purpose of promoting an exhibition to receive their reimbursement before profits are distributed.

Some galleries will pay for or partially pay for additional support materials such as catalogs, brochures or biography sheets. This is to your benefit, but remember, they will likely not want to absorb the expense of these materials by taking it from the profits of the exhibition. Make sure this is agreed on ahead of time.

Payment for art works sold are usually received within thirty days of the sale unless you stipulate other arrangements ahead of time. It is not unheard of to request your share in the sale a few days after the collector's check clears the bank. These details should all be covered in your contractual agreements ahead of time.

Museums generally cover the expenses of shipping and insuring art work both to and from the exhibition. These venues are not in the business of selling art but of exhibiting art for the enrichment of the communities. Museums will provide the necessary loan agreements, insurance documents, condition reports, and all other supportive documents required for their purposes. Other academic venues vary in their policies regarding the expenses they will cover, so make sure you ask at the onset what your responsibility is.

Standard Documentation and Legal Forms

As an artist, you will have to undertake the responsibility of signing contracts and agreements pertaining to your work. It is wise for you to have some idea of what elements should be present in a good contract. Even so, have an attorney review all agreements before you submit or sign them. Know what you are obligating yourself to.

All contracts should include the specific names of ***both parties*** who are making the agreement, the signed consent of each listed party, the monetary or material consideration that will be made as a result of this agreement, and a detailed description of the obligation or actions being agreed to. The following standard contracts are discussed in this chapter.

Bill of Sale
Certificate of Authenticity
Provenance
Exhibition Agreement/Loan Agreement
Artist/Gallery Consignment Agreement
Condition Report
Insurance Agreement
Artwork Documentation for the Artist

Contract Summary

✓ **Bill of Sale**

Who: Provided to the purchaser of any work at the time of sale.
What: Serves as a receipt and record for the transfer of funds for the ownership of an art work. Notifies the purchaser of the artist's retainment of the rights for reproduction.
When: Any time a purchase of work occurs.

✓ **Certificate of Authenticity**

Who: Provided to the purchaser of any work at the time of sale. (Some states permit the artist to provide this certificate after the sale. Consult with your state's regulations.)
What: Proof from the artist to the purchaser of the authenticity of the piece as a work of art by the artist as represented during the sale of the art.
When: Any time a purchase of work occurs.

✓ **Provenance**

Who: Provided to the purchaser of any work at the time of sale.
What: Documents the history of the piece, the transition of ownership from person to person, and the exhibition places of the piece. A chronological documentation of the exposure and ownership of a work of art.
When: Any time a purchase of work occurs.

✓ **Agent Representation Contract**

Who: Provided for and to the artist when representation is obtained.
What: Documents and confirms all obligations of the representative to the artist and vice versa, formalizing the relationship and reimbursements criteria.
When: When representation is agreed upon and prior to the beginning of any activity in accordance with this relationship.

✓ Exhibition Agreement/Loan Agreement

Who: Provided for and to the artist when art work is to be transferred for the purpose of exhibition or sale.
What: Documents the transfer of location of art work without the transfer of ownership. Often provided to the artist by, for example, the museum. Should be used prior to the transfer of location for any exhibition.
When: Prior to the shipment of art work to an exhibition location.

✓ Artist/Gallery Consignment Agreement

Who: Provided for and to the artist when art work is consigned for sale to a venue.
What: Documents the transfer of location of art work for the purpose of sale without the transfer of ownership. Often provided to the artist by the gallery. Should be used prior to the transfer of location for any exhibition.
When: At the time of delivery to the gallery.

✓ Condition Report

Who: Provided by the artist to the venue, usually a museum, at the time of shipment.
What: Documents in detail the complete condition of the art work at the time of shipment; scratches, chips, cleanliness of the piece, any damage or lack of damage.
When: Created at the time of delivery to the museum by the museum, and at the time of departure, noting the condition of the work at that time. Usually conducted by the museum registrar.

✓ Insurance Agreement

Who: Provided by the artist or the venue, whichever party who has agreed to take responsibility for insuring the work in transit.
What: Documents insurance of the art work during transit.
When: Prior to the crating and shipment of art work.

Bill of Sale

Place: ______________________________
(Gallery, museum, art show, studio address or business)

Sold To: ______________________________
(Name of Buyer)

____
(Address of Buyer)

____
(Phone Number of Buyer)

Sold By: ______________________________
(Name of Seller -- Artist or Authorized Dealer)

____
(Address of Seller)

____
(Phone Number of Seller)

Description of Work: ______________________________
(Title)

____
(Subject, Media, Dimensions)

____
(Description)

Price: ______________________________
(Complete Purchase Price)

Terms of Payment: ______________________________

____

REPRODUCTION RIGHTS RESERVED BY THE ARTIST

____
(Purchaser's Signature)

____
(Artist or Authorized Dealer's Signature)

Date: ______________________________

Certificate of Authenticity

Artist: ______________________________

Title: ______________________________

Media: ______________________________

Dimensions: ______________________________

Year: ______________________________

Comments: ______________________________

____

This is to certify that the artwork described above and attached hereto is an original work by the named artist.

______________________________ ______________

(Artist or Authorized Dealer's Signature) (Date)

Certificate of Authenticity

Artist: ______________________________

Title: ______________________________

Media: ______________________________

Dimensions: ______________________________

Publisher: ______________________________

Year: __________

No. of authorized signed prints in this edition: ___
No. of artist proofs: ___
No. of unsigned proofs: ___

No. of other editions: ___
Size of other editions: ___

Comments: ______________________________

____

This is to certify that the artwork described above and attached hereto is an original print by the named artist.

____
(Artist or Authorized Representative Signature)

____
(Date)

Provenance

This document serves as first issue of Provenance

Type of Art: ______________________

Artist: ______________________

Place Image Here

Title: ______________________

Dimensions: ______________________

Year: ____________

This artwork was completed by the artist in __________ and was signed and so designated by the artist as to the year of completion and authenticity.

This artwork was acquired by ______________________ in ____________.
(Seller) (Year of Purchase)

Ownership of the above described work was transferred to:

____
(Name of Buyer)

____
(Address of Buyer)

____
(Phone Number of Buyer)

on ____________, 19___ for the sum of: ______________________ ($______________).
(Sale Date) (Purchase Price)

As of this date, ownership of this painting remains with ______________________.

____ ______________
(Seller's Signature) (Date)

Exhibition Agreement

This "Exhibition Agreement" is made and entered into to be effective as of the __________ day of ________________________ 19___, by and between ______________________________, sometimes referred to as "Artist" and ______________________________ sometimes referred to as "Authorized Representative" providing exhibition space for the works described hereto, sometimes referred to as "Space."

The purpose of this agreement is to set forth the understandings governing the agreed to exhibition by Artist of the described works of art in the Exhibition Space.

Artist:

____
(Name of Artist)

____
(Address)

____
(Telephone)

Exhibition Space:

____
(Name of Space)

____
(Location of Space)

____
(Authorized Representative for Space)

Artworks for Exhibition:

Title	Media	Dimensions	Year

Duration: ____________________ to ____________________
(Starting Date of Exhibition) (Ending Date of Exhibition)

____
(Exhibition Hours Open to the Public)

No works shall be removed from the Space's premises until sold or returned to the Artist, unless otherwise agreed upon in writing.

Page 1 of 3

Installation: Artist / Space (circle one) shall be solely responsible for the installation of the exhibition. Installation shall begin on _____________, 19___ and be completed by _____________, 19___. All final installation decisions shall be the sole responsibility of the Space staff. Materials required for installation, including mountings, tape, pins, nails, etc. as required are the responsibility of the Artist / Space (circle one).

Delivery: Artworks are to arrive at the Space on _____________, 19___ by ______ am/pm. Artworks shall be confirmed as received by ________________.

Shipment of the works to the Space shall be arranged by ________________ and paid for by ____________________________ including insurance. Artist shall advise the Space in writing of the prices and insurance values for each work to be exhibited by ____________, 19___.

Insurance: Space shall insure the works for the values assigned by the Artist from the period when the works arrive at the Space until the works are removed from the Space. The Space is responsible for security of all works while present on the Space premises. The Space represents that it is in sound repair and shall be responsible for damage to the works as a result of structural defects, water damage, vandalism, theft or the like. The Space shall exercise reasonable care in dealing with the works.

The Space shall maintain all public and exhibition areas in a good state of repair, clean and orderly.

Promotions: The following publicity and promotions shall be provided for this exhibition:

__	Invitations	Artist / Space / Shared
__	Press Releases	Artist / Space / Shared
__	Public Service Announcements	Artist / Space / Shared
__	Advertisements	Artist / Space / Shared
__	Posters	Artist / Space / Shared
__	Brochure / Catalog	Artist / Space / Shared
__	Artists Reception	Artist / Space / Shared
__	Other ______________	Artist / Space / Shared

The costs of promotions shall be reimbursed to the Artist and/or Space as agreed upon hereto:

____

____

____

____

Page 2 of 3

Deinstallation: Artist / Space (circle one) shall be solely responsible for the deinstallation of the exhibition. Deinstallation shall begin on _____________, 19___ and be completed by _____________, 19___.

Artworks not sold during the exhibition are to be returned to the artist by _____________, 19___ by ______ am/pm. Return shipment of the works will be arranged by __________________ and paid for by ___________________________, including insurance based on the values provided at time of delivery.

Remuneration: In remuneration for exhibiting and selling the Artist's works, the Space shall receive a ______% commission on the Net / Gross (circle one) sale of the art.

For commissions based on net sales values, the following expenses shall be subtracted from the sale revenues prior to determining the total commission to be paid the Space:

____

____

Artist is to receive the monies from the sale of the work within _____ days of receipt from the purchaser. Delinquency in payment will activate a __ % penalty to be subtracted from the Space's commission.

Amendments: Amendments, modifications, supplements or changes to this Agreement shall be in writing and signed by both parties.

Termination of Agreement by Both Parties: Either party may terminate this Agreement by giving to the other party sixty (60) days notice in writing.

Laws Governing Agreement: This agreement shall be governed by and construed in accordance with the laws of the State of ________________.

Both parties agree that this represents the entire understanding between them, and that it shall be a binding contract upon the signature of the Artist and an authorized representative of the Space.

____ ______________

(Artist or Authorized Dealer's Signature) (Date)

____ ______________

(Authorized Space Representative) (Date)

Page 3 of 3

Consignment Agreement

It is hereby agreed between ____, hereinafter referred to as "owner" of the art works described in Schedule A, attached hereto, and ____, hereinafter referred to as "dealer", that dealer shall exhibit and offer the described art work for sale to dealer's clients under the following conditions:

1. The works hereby consigned to the dealer as agent for the owner and described herein are priced at net to owner on the attached list. All works shall remain the property of the owner unless and until they are purchased by collectors or the dealer.

2. The works shall be exhibited, or made available for inspection by prospective purchasers, by the dealer from ________________, 19___ until this agreement is terminated by owner or dealer upon 30 days written notice to the other party.

3. The owner will assist the dealer by framing all works hereby consigned. The owner's incurred costs in framing will be returned to the owner in addition to the sale price of the work of art.

4. The dealer will pay the owner the net price hereby established and agreed upon per the attached inventory sheet on any works sold by the dealer. Notice of all sales will be given to the owner at the conclusion of each month and payment of all monies due shall be made not more than thirty days after the receipt of payment by the dealer. The dealer assumes full risk of nonpayment by the purchaser.

5. During the term of this agreement and during shipping from and to the owner, the dealer shall cause all of owner's work consigned to the dealer to be insured to the benefit of owner against any and all loss in an amount equal to the owner's net amount.

6. No unsold works shall be removed from the dealer's premises until the works are sold to a purchaser unless agreed upon in writing.

7. The owner shall have the right to inventory all consigned works at reasonable times and to obtain a full accounting for any works not present at the dealer's premises at such time.

8. The owner, as copyright owner of the hereby consigned works, reserves all rights to the reproduction of the works in any manner. This restriction shall be indicated by the dealer in writing on all sales invoices and memoranda. However, the owner will not withhold permission for the reproduction of such works for promotional purposes if all such reproductions are submitted to owner for approval prior to any printing and distribution of said promotional materials.

Page 1 of 3

9. This agreement shall at all times be governed by the laws of the state of ___________.

____ ______________
(Artist's Signature) (Date)

____
(Artist's Printed Name)

____
(Artist's Street Address)

____
(Artist's City, State, Zip, and Country Address)

____
(Artist's Telephone Number(s))

____ ______________
(Authorized Representative's Signature) (Date)

____
(Authorized Representative's Printed Name)

____
(Venue Name)

____
(Venue Street Address)

____
(Venue City, State, Zip, and Country Address)

____
(Venue Telephone Number(s))

Schedule A

Total Number of Pieces Consigned under This Agreement: ___________

[__] ______________________________ ____________
(Title) (Year Created)

____
(Subject, Media, Dimensions)

____
(Description)

[__] ______________________________ ____________
(Title) (Year Created)

____
(Subject, Media, Dimensions)

____
(Description)

[__] ______________________________ ____________
(Title) (Year Created)

____
(Subject, Media, Dimensions)

____
(Description)

[__] ______________________________ ____________
(Title) (Year Created)

____
(Subject, Media, Dimensions)

____
(Description)

[__] ______________________________ ____________
(Title) (Year Created)

____
(Subject, Media, Dimensions)

____
(Description)

[__] ______________________________ ____________
(Title) (Year Created)

____
(Subject, Media, Dimensions)

____
(Description)

Page 3 of 3

Condition Report

Name of Lender: ____

Name of Institution: ____

Address: ____

City: ______________________________ State: ________ Zip Code: ____________

Artist: ____

Title: ____

Dimensions: ____

Media: ____

Year: ______________________

This report is to document the condition of the above described artwork at this time of receipt ____________, 19___ by the institution.

__ Condition of Frame: ____
____
____

__ Condition of paint, canvas, etc. indicating any minor blemishes.
____
____

__ Report any abnormal condition of the artwork:
____
____

Indicate by photo or diagram any and all suspicious or damaged areas. Attach said documentation to this report and lender's copy. Immediately notify lender of damage.

____ ____________________________
(Registrar's Signature) (Institution)

Artwork Documentation for the Artist

Type of Work: ________________ Category: ________________ Catalog No: _______

Artist: ____

Title: ____

Description: ____

Size: ________________ Medium: ____________________ Completion Date: _______

Date Acquired by ______________________: _____________ Framed: __ Yes __ No

Exhibits:

______________________________ __________ to __________
(Location) (Dates of Exhibition)

______________________________ __________ to __________

______________________________ __________ to __________

Scholarship: __ Yes __ No

Condition Report on File: __ Yes __ No

Estimated Value: $_____________

Appraisal Value: $_____________

Place Image Here

Date Sold: _______________

Name of Buyer: ________________

Address: ____________________

City: _________________________

State: ___ Zip Code: ______

Sales Price: $____________

PROMOTIONS

Your goal in promoting your work is to arouse the interest of the art community about your work, to move them to action, to come see and experience your work, and to talk to others about it. You will employ a variety of means to create this excitement ranging from printed materials, printed and electronic press, special events, to personal networking. Many of your options are not expensive but simply require ingenuity and perseverance on your part.

Artists often are intimidated by the idea of promoting their work. The process you have undertaken to qualify and present your work to venues has been a form of promotion. You have been spreading the word to a focused audience. Promotions on a grander scale simply broadens this audience. Once you have achieved a goal, it is time to tell the world that something very exciting is happening. You must arouse the interest and curiosity of the art community to come see and experience your work. An artist in a bubble will never achieve the level of recognition his or her art is worthy of. Do not rely solely on others to make it happen for you. Stay on top of what is happening.

Who Is Responsible for Promotions?

You are! It is your art and the success of your career that is at issue. You must actively participate in this process. You will find that many venues are willing and able to take responsibility for promoting their events, but be ready to pitch in creatively, actively, and in some cases, financially. You want to take advantage of any and all exposure. Do not expect everyone to be capable of achieving the quality of promotion of your works as you want done.

There are different levels of promoting. One level deals with an immediate need. Your activities will be focused on a shorter term goal, for example, an upcoming exhibition. Another level of promotion deals with your personal long-term goals, for example, raising the importance of your art to such a level as to make it worthy of academic exhibitions, such as in museums. Different activities are undertaken to achieve both types of goals.

Before You Begin -- Keys to Promotional Success

Before you actually begin any promotional program, there are a few rules to keep in mind.

Organization Starting out and staying organized will be the key to success. Plan each promotional activity carefully, taking into consideration the timing and cost of each step in your plan. Use the checklist provided to organize what needs to be done. This will keep you on top of the game.

Know Your Audience

Certain types of promotional activities will be more cost effective and give you better results than others depending on the audience you have selected. Know your audience. Avoid using the "shotgun" approach to distributing your materials. It is important to know where and why your materials are being presented to the individuals within your selected audience.

Mailing Lists

Keep a current mailing list of all people who have expressed interest in or collected your work. Include in your list local art writers or critics, targeted venue staff members, members of the press, influential art patrons and members of the art community who are "in the spotlight." The mailing lists will be continuously updated with new names and new information.

Resources for obtaining mailing lists can be found in a variety of places. For example, review the names listed in your guest book from an exhibition. Specialized mailing lists can be purchased from publications and organizations. Local nonprofit organizations are a good example of these specialized lists. The wife of one artist whom I work with estimates she can count on three to four purchases from people on her sales list rather than just one. She maintains a constant communication with her collectors by cultivating her list.

Mailing lists are most easily kept on a computer so that you can print labels by categories quickly and easily. There are many reasonably priced software packages on the market designed for just such purposes. **Even if you don't have access to a computer, you must keep the lists up to date.**

Follow Up

Following up on your activities is imperative. Personal contact with your audience will always enhance the effectiveness of your promotion. For example, when you send a press release to a local writer or critic, it is best if you also make a call to confirm receipt of the materials and to answer any questions. You may wish to take advantage of the opportunity to personally invite them yourself to the opening reception.

Perseverance

At first you may feel as if your efforts are not being rewarded but, in time, the barriers will come down. Observe the responses you are getting from your materials, adjust what needs to be adjusted, and simply keep at it. Keep an open mind and learn from each activity. You will eventually become part of the mainstream art community.

Promotions for Scheduled Events

Invitations, press releases, public service announcements, editorials, posters, tear sheets, catalogs, and brochures are all promotional materials that can be used to elicit interest in scheduled events. Each item is used for a different purpose and is directed to a different audience. Plan to utilize one or more of these techniques to advertise your event.

Invitations

Invitations are mailed out to entice people to come to your show. You should direct an invitation to members of the art community including university faculty, museum curators and directors, gallery dealers, art organizations, collectors, general patrons, etc. These are the people who will "talk up" the event for you.

An invitation can take on almost any form and can range greatly in price. If you have a large budget, you can print a card with a full-color image of a piece from your show on one side and invitational information on the other. Avoid being gimmicky or "cutesy". The invitation, as should all your other materials, should reflect upon you as a professional and not be too slick or glitzy.

Cost-effective Invitation Format

It is my opinion, however, that there are many other alternatives you can use that will allow you to apply your funds to something more permanent, such as your catalog or brochure. An invitation will be used for a single event whereas the catalog or brochure will be used again and again to build your career. A cost-effective and impressive invitation can be made from an 8-1/2" x 11" piece of paper properly formatted, printed, and folded. A sample of this cost-effective invitation is shown on the following pages.

The idea behind this invitation design is to fold the page so that it ends up looking like a fold-over card. Use a small white or colored sticker to hold the invitation closed. Once the invitation is received, the sticker will be sliced or removed to open and read the inside. You can use little "special touches" to give greater sophistication to this invitation design, but remember to keep away from becoming too commercial looking unless that is the marketplace you are approaching.

You may consider using a full-color versus a black-and-white image on your invitation. Color is preferred, but don't be upset if black and white is what your budget allows for. Your venue may have an invitation budget for the exhibition. You may wish to contribute to this budget to upgrade the quality of the invitation, for example, from a black-and-white image to a color image; be creative.

When to Mail the Invitation

Invitations are generally mailed out two weeks prior to the opening dates of the exhibition. If mailed too soon, the invitations may get lost; too late, people will have already made plans. In planning when to send your invitations, consider how long the mail will take to deliver the piece. Mail moves more quickly in some areas than in others.

BRUMSCHMELT GALLERY
5930 Michaelson Drive
Los Angeles, CA 90013

JEROME GASTALDI

"Television Autocracy"

October 18 through November 28, 1992

Artist's Reception:
Sunday, October 18th, 2-5pm, at the

BRUMSCHMELT GALLERY
5930 Michaelson Drive
Los Angeles, CA 90013

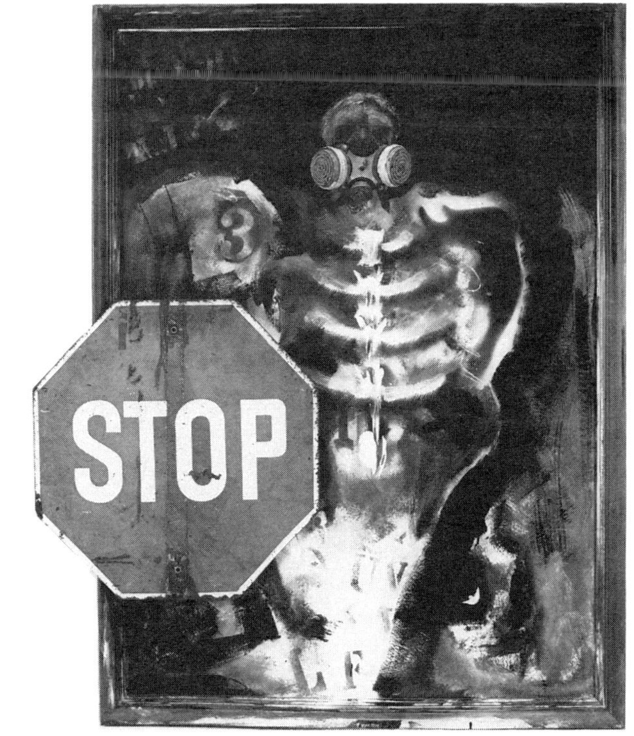

Swan Dive Highway (53" x 39")

(213) 617-7891
Gallery hours: Tues. - Sat. 11-5pm

Invitation Worksheet

(Your Name) *JEROME GASTALDI*

(Event Name) *"Television Autocracy"*

(Event Dates) *October 18 - November 28, 1992*

Insert Your Image Here

Artist's Reception:
(Day, Date, Time) *Sunday, October 18th, 2-5pm*

(Location Name) *BRUMSCHMELT GALLERY*
(Location Address) *5930 Michaelson Drive*
Los Angeles, CA 90013

(Contact Phone) *(213) 617-7891*
(Daily Hours) *Tues. - Sat. 11 - 5 pm*

(Image Title) *"Swan Dive Highway" (53" x 39")*

Press Releases

The press release is used to inform newspapers, art writers, art critics, art magazines, and other social and educational publications about your exhibition. It is most effective to direct the press release to two or three individuals within each targeted newspaper or magazine. These people rely on press releases to keep them up to date on the news to print. Your gallery may be experienced in dealing with the press, but make sure they are sending out what you want projected. The press release should be directed from the exhibiting venue to the press and not from the artist. I think it is important to know at all times what is being stated about you and your work.

Create a list of all newspapers and magazines distributed in the geographical areas you wish to target. Local press associations often publish inexpensive booklets which can be found in your local library, with this information completely outlined. Review your list and remove any publications that do not cover the art community. Your list should now be down to a manageable size, anywhere from ten to thirty publications depending on the population of your targeted community.

For each publication, identify the two or three people who cover the art scene. This may include an art critic, an art editor, a community events editor, a managing editor, or the chief editor. Call each publication to determine who handles press releases for upcoming art events. Ask for the proper spelling of his or her name, exact title, and the address to mail the release to. Once you have this information, add them to your "press" mailing list.

Format of a Press Release

A press release is written in a succinct fashion with all the key information very clearly stated. Include the following information:

"Press Release"
Name of the Venue
Venue Phone Number
Name of the Venue Representative
Title of the Venue Representative

Venue Address
Venue Operating Hours

Artist Name(s)
Event Name
Event Dates
Artist Reception Day, Date and Time

Brief Statement About the Event
Brief Statement About the Artist(s)

Avoid using flowery language within your press release. Keep your approach simple. The press appreciate concise, clear writing. For best results, laser print the release as you would any other presentation piece, and make the additional copies on a quality photocopier.

Mail the press release in an 8-1/2" x 11" envelope, addressed with typed or printed labels. Do not fold your press release. Use the return address of the venue and not your own.

When to Mail the Press Release

Each publication will have its own deadline date. Magazines often stop accepting releases two to three months prior to the publication. Newspapers are far more flexible with their deadline dates, generally two weeks prior to the publication date. As you call each publication to identify the proper contacts, ask what their deadline dates are for submitting a press release. Note this on your list. You may even choose to organize your press list in order of deadline dates.

Send a Photograph

For the art writers and critics and those editorial type magazines that commonly print art works, include one or two of your strong 8" x 10" or 8-1/2" x 11" black-and-white prints. When it comes down to the time they put together their final copy and they are looking to fill space with a photo, you may benefit by being prepared so they don't have to send a staff photographer out to shoot your work, saving both time and money. Do not go to the great expense of enclosing a photograph with every press release. Select those key press contacts whose publications print art works.

Always properly label the picture in case it becomes separated from your package. I also recommend using a sheet of paper laser printed with my name, title of the painting, a brief statement about the exhibition, exhibition dates, location, and contact phone number taped to the photograph just as it would appear in the newspaper. This information makes it very easy to use the print. A sample of a photograph prepared this way is shown on the following pages.

LOS ANGELES CONTEMPORARY ARTS

NEWS RELEASE
For additional information, contact:
Jie Shim, Director (213) 381-1525

EXHIBITION "GASTALDI"

LOS ANGELES, California - A one-man exhibition of fine art by the artist, Jerome Gastaldi, opens at the Los Angeles Contemporary Arts Gallery, Los Angeles, California on June 15th and runs through July 3rd, 1992. This exhibition will feature recent works including his paintings with integrated video monitors playing his productions.

A reception for the artist is scheduled for the evening of Friday, June 19th from 6:00 p.m. to 9:00 p.m..

JEROME GASTALDI

Gastaldi was born in Oakland, California, in 1945. He is a painter and a mixed media artist. Gastaldi's 10' x 8' integrated video painting, ***Electronic Blessing Whether You Like It or Not,*** includes nine television monitors in the shape of a cross all playing a video of a Catholic priest giving a blessing. The piece was selected for the international exhibition, ***Images Du Futur 1992*** in Montreal, Canada which opened May, 1992. He will also be showing at the Southern California Art Institute in Orange County from June 11th through July 10th and at the South Bay Contemporary Museum in Torrance, California from June 27th through August 6th.

The Los Angeles Contemporary Arts Gallery (LACA) is located at 3630 Wilshire Blvd., Los Angeles, California 90010. Telephone (213) 381-1525.

Gallery hours are 11:00 a.m. to 7:00 p.m., Monday through Saturday.

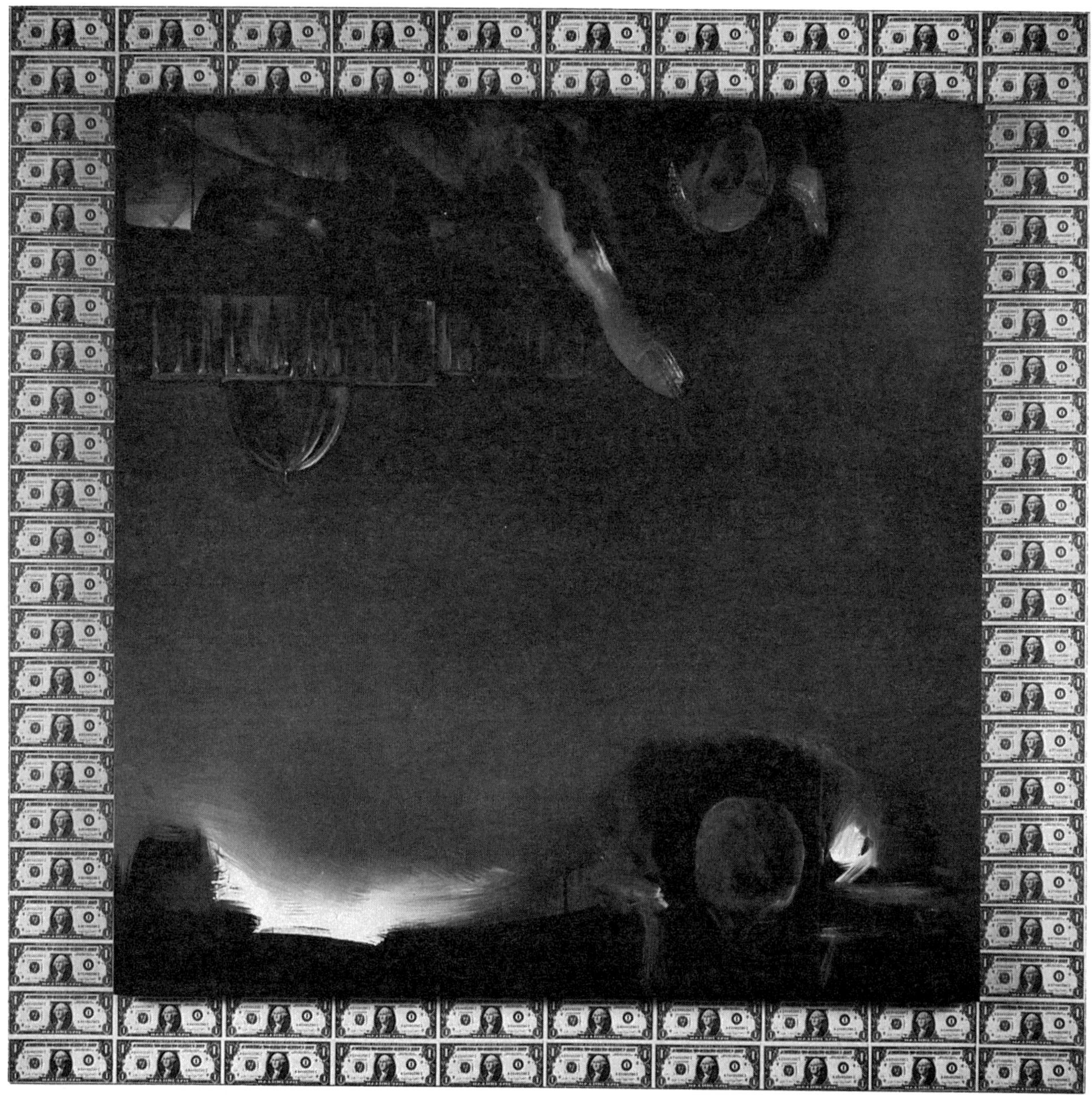

JEROME GASTALDI , "ONE NATION OVER GOD" is a featured work at the one man exhibition of paintings, sculpture and integrated video paintings opening June 15th at Los Angeles Contemporary Arts Gallery (LACA). The exhibition runs through July 3rd.

LOS ANGELES CONTEMPORARY ARTS

Press Release Worksheet

(Venue Name) *Los Angeles Contemporary Arts*

NEWS RELEASE

For additional information, contact:

(Contact Name) *Jie Shim, Director*
(Contact Phone Number) *(213) 381-1525*

(Artist Last Name or Exhibition Name) *"GASTALDI"*

(City, State Location) *Los Angeles, CA*

(Brief Statement About Event) *A one-man exhibition of f.a. by the artist, JG, opens at the Los Angeles Contemporary Arts Gallery, Los Angeles, California on June 15th and runs through July 3rd, 1992. This exhibition will feature recent works including his paintings with integrated video monitors playing his productions.*

(Event Dates) *June 15th through July 3rd, 1992*

(Reception Day, Date, Time) *Friday, June 19th, 6:00pm to 9:00pm*

(Brief Artist Statement) *G born Oakland, CA, 1945. Painter and mixed media artist. G's 10' x 8' integrated video painting, Electronic Blessing...., nine television monitors in the shape of a cross al playing a video of a Catholic priest giving a blessing. The piece selected Intl. exh., Images du Futur 1992, Montreal, Canada, opened May, 1992. Also showing SCAI in OC from June 11th through July 10th and SBCM in Torrance, CA from June 27th through Aug 6th.*

(Venue Name -- Repeated) *The Los Angeles Contemporary Arts Gallery (LACA)*
(Complete Venue Address) *3630 Wilshire Blvd., Los Angeles, CA 90010 (213) 381-1525*

(Venue Hours) *M - Sat, 11:00am - 7:00pm*

Format the text to emphasize the key pieces of information.

Public Service Announcements

Many artists do not realize the ease with which you can promote an event through the radio and television. Like the print publications, many stations have public service announcements regarding events occurring in their audience's area.

Create a list of all the radio and television stations whose broadcasts focus on the geographic area you are interested in approaching. Don't overlook the local college and university stations. Again, local press associations often publish inexpensive booklets which can be found in your local public library with this information completely outlined. Review your list and remove any stations whose programming is not aimed at the type of audience you wish to alert, for example, children's programming.

For each station, identify the person who coordinates the public service announcements. This may include a station manager or the public services coordinator. Call the station to determine who handles the public service announcements. Ask for the proper spelling of his or her name, exact title, and the address to mail the announcement to. Oftentimes, the station will instruct you to facsimile the announcement. Once you have this information, add it to your "press" list.

Format of a Public Service Announcement

The major stations have press kits for writing public service announcements. Request that a kit be sent to you at least one month before you are ready to approach the station. The rules for writing, presentation, and clarity we followed for the press release also apply to the public service announcement.

When to Facsimile the Public Service Announcement

Each station will have its own deadline date, generally, one to two weeks prior to the event. As you contact each station, ask what the deadline dates are for submitting a public service announcement. Note this on your list.

Editorial -- Free Press with a Punch

Receiving editorial review is not as difficult as one might think. It requires a good package with a "hook" or something about your exhibition that is different. This will inspire the writer to learn more about you and your work. Personal contact and rapport with the critic or writer you wish to have review your work is also helpful. Do not be afraid to contact the writer; all he or she can say is no. Push your gallery to do the work of contacting the press as well.

This type of promotion takes planning. Begin by sending a press release to the writer. Follow it up with a personal phone call inviting him or her to attend your reception. Send a follow-up invitation as a reminder of your gesture. If the writer would like to see your exhibit, be available. Your gallery should be helpful in making the contact as well, but do not rely on it.

Be attentive. Introduce the writer to your dealer if they do not already know each other. If you have a catalog or brochure, give a signed copy to the writer. After the show, send the writer a thank-you note for attending.

Establishing rapport with a writer can open up new opportunities. Do not directly ask the writer to write about your show. Let your dealer be the one who pushes. Even if you are involved behind the scenes, you do not want the writer to get the impression you are trying to promote yourself.

Posters

Posters are specifically designed to spread the word about an event. The use of the posters is popular in metropolitan areas such as New York, where you see them pasted in every conceivable location. Some galleries and museums also use the poster as another product to sell at an exhibition as it lends to the perceived credibility of the artist to the public.

Format of a Poster

The format of a poster is "anything goes." There are many books written on how to design and print successful posters. The idea is to spark the interest of the viewer to such a degree that they come to your event. Intrigue the viewer with the poster. Remember to include the event dates and location on the poster. Many people like to collect exhibition posters as they are affordable to most anyone. You can produce a black-and-white poster on a limited budget that can be quite effective.

Be a Considerate Artist

Once printed, paste the poster up all around town. Paste it up in places where posters are acceptable. Ask shopkeepers if you may put one of your posters in their window. Go to popular "hangouts", colleges, restaurants, and the like. Ask permission to hang one of your posters in their establishment. Canvasing the community requires mostly leg work.

Do not violate any city ordinances or impose on the private property of others. Some cities require a permit to display posters.

Special Events

Everyone likes a party and a smart artist will know how to use this to his or her benefit. There are a number of events that you can hold to bring the art community in to see your work. The most common event is an artist's reception held on the opening day of an exhibition. This can be a simple reception with refreshments or something more elaborate.

You can also use other types of events to promote your work.

Charity Events

Charity events, including auctions, dinners, fund-raisers and the like, are excellent opportunities for you to have your work seen. Donate your work to worthy causes. Patrons of such events tend to be in tune with the art world and will be interested in the art for their own personal collections. It can open up future possibilities for you.

Open House at Your Studio

An open house at your studio is an invitation to come see your art in your work environment. It can be arranged much like an artist's reception. The type of open house you hold may reflect the type of art you create. Be creative and you will find that your budget will go far.

An open house should not be held too frequently, possibly two times a year. Depending upon the area you live in -- for example, a metropolitan area versus a more rural area -- entertaining by an artist may be done more or less frequently. You may want to team up with a dealer because it is easier for the dealer to work the sale while you entertain your guests.

Use your mailing list. Many collectors like to go to the artist's studio to meet the artist and see what new pieces are available and ones that are being worked on. You may opt to invite a specific individual or let it be a drop-by and informal visit format. Be sure to mail personal invitations to your guests well in advance of your event. Do not notify the press of your open house. It may be perceived as too "happy-hands-at-home."

Be selective about what art pieces you show. Have only your strongest pieces, and possibly a few in the process of being created, out for your guests to view. Put away any pieces that are not part of your current body of work, as it may confuse your guests about your work. Recall the lessons learned by the artist who showed the dealer his entire collection of works and was subsequently rebuffed.

Demonstrations at Art Fairs / Public Places

Commercial artists can use demonstrations at art fairs and expositions to put themselves before the public. The idea is to be out in front of the public attending the art event. You never know who may be interested in purchasing your work or what dealers will offer you an opportunity to exhibit in their galleries.

Lectures

The fine artist can use a similar opportunity to get exposure by lecturing at colleges, universities, art organizations, and the like. Feel free to write a brief press release about your upcoming lecture. The press always picks up on events like this.

Long-term Promotional Options

Once again, there are different levels of promoting. One level deals with an immediate need. Your activities are focused on a short-term goal, for example, an upcoming exhibition. Another level of promotion deals with your personal long-term goals, for example, raising the importance of your art to such a level as to make it worthy of a museum exhibition. Different activities can be undertaken to achieve your long-term goals. Always keep your long-term goals in mind.

Newsletters

A newsletter is a relatively inexpensive way to keep your audience abreast of the progression of your career. It allows you to talk about new works, published works, upcoming events, awards and honors you have received to just about anything you feel your audience will be interested in knowing about.

An artist's newsletter should be academic in form. Many good books have been published on the subject of newsletters, providing numerous examples. Invest a few dollars in one of these books to keep at your desk for reference.

Mail a newsletter to each of the people on your mailing list. Have copies of the most recent letter available as hand out material at your exhibitions and at your representative galleries. You may consider sending a copy to your press contacts as well. The newsletter is a promotional tool to keep your name and your work in front of the people.

A word of caution: when writing a newsletter, be careful not to make it sound like a vanity piece. The language should not be boastful but informative and interesting. Have someone whose opinion you respect, read and critique your letter before you go to final print and begin distribution.

Newsletters do not necessarily have to be printed by a professional print shop. If you have access to a computer with a laser printer and a desktop publishing software package, you can prepare an impressive publication. Print the first copy on your laser printer, then take that over to a copy service to be photocopied. You can make the newsletter as elaborate or as simple as you wish. The key will be to give the recipient the impression that this is a professional's publication and the information interesting and worthwhile to read.

Videos

In this age of electronic media, many artists have begun to produce videos about themselves and their works. These are short presentations designed to give the viewer an understanding of the artist and their works.

If you are interested in producing a video, I strongly advise you consult with a production company that is knowledgeable about artists' promotional videos. Using a homemade video for promotion can give the impression of amateurism.

The cost of producing videos can be expensive, when properly done. I advise holding off on this type of project until you have a budget for it. You will not want to take too many shortcuts in producing your video, as the professionalism can easily be lost. Consider using the resources of your local college or university to keep the costs down. This can also give a student a valuable experience for their career.

Advertising

Advertising, as with the video, can be quite expensive. There are many options you can use to promote yourself without going to such expense. But, if you feel you need to advertise your work in a magazine or newspaper, I suggest consulting a person familiar with targeting your market to help you design and place your advertisements.

You will want to plan carefully when and where your advertisements will be placed. An advertising person familiar with the art market and the art publications should be able to direct you to negotiating a good location for your ad in the magazine. Covers, inside and out, are more expensive than advertisements within the body of the publication.

I have discussed the benefits of advertising with many dealers. Most feel that the only thing they received out of advertising was name recognition. You cannot advertise only once or twice. It must be on a regular basis. I recommend spending your promotional dollars on other options unless you are aided by your venue. I do not recommend putting an advertisement in a magazine or newspaper with your phone and address as it looks too self-promotional.

Submitting Articles to Publications

If your writing skills are proficient or you can partner up with someone whose are, you may consider submitting articles to various magazines. These articles can discuss your work, issues confronted by your work, events and benefits supported by your work, or any topic that is appropriate to the focus of the magazine you are submitting to. The process of having an article accepted by a magazine can be frustrating. But if you persevere, you will eventually have success.

Television and Radio Shows

Now we are talking about the artist who is really willing to put it all on the line. If you are, you should begin to research which news and talk shows focus segments on the arts. In my area, for example, there is a public television show funded by a grant from a regional arts foundation. Its focus is to inform and enlighten the community about the arts. This could be a good candidate for you to research. Metropolitan areas abound with these types of shows. Television interviews are also an inexpensive way to have a video made about you and your work. Consider approaching the local cable stations and television or radio stations at your local universities.

Begin by sending a public service announcement to the show's producer. Then, in a fashion similar to your standard venue presentation, you will begin to solicit the show. Learn about its focus, what it is trying to achieve. Watch the show to see what kind of people and events are covered. Develop your presentation to correspond to this focus. Be willing to be persistent.

Your Options Are Limitless

When you are promoting yourself, have a plan and stick to it. At times you will need to step back, regroup and then proceed on with your plan. The options you have to promote yourself are limited only by your imagination. Above all else, network in the community. Be seen.

Your only limitations are your expectations.

CAREER PLAN

Promotional Schedule

Four Months Prior to Exhibition:

✓ Confirm exhibition details (participants, dates, opening reception, location, etc.).
✓ Design and print press releases.
✓ Submit press releases to magazines (longer deadline publications).

Three Months Prior to Exhibition:

✓ Design and be prepared to print invitations.
✓ Design catalogs, brochures, etc. for the exhibition.

Two Months Prior to Exhibition:

✓ Design and print posters (optional).

One Month Prior to Exhibition:

✓ Print invitations.
✓ Print catalog, brochure or other printed materials.
✓ Begin soliciting editorial review for your exhibition (dealer involvement).
✓ Plan details of the opening event (catering, music, vip arrangements, etc.).

Two Weeks Prior to Exhibition:

✓ Deliver public service announcements to radio and television stations.
✓ Mail invitations.
✓ Mail press releases to newspapers, art writers and art critics (with and without attached photographs).
✓ Begin follow-up calls. (You will increase your attendance ten-fold with personal contact.)
✓ Arrange for a photographer (professional or amateur) to be present at opening.

One Week Prior to Exhibition:

✓ Continue follow-up calls.

Day of Exhibition:

✓ Attend the artist's reception.

Follow Up:

✓ Send thank-you notes to key patrons of event.
✓ Update your mailing list with new people and corrected information.
✓ Follow up personally with those who expressed interest in purchasing your work. (Dealer should be involved.)
✓ Invite interested people to your gallery or studio.

CAREER PLAN

Promotion Checklist

To obtain the most from your promotional dollar, it is important to have a plan. Use this worksheet to select the types of promotions you wish to use in your plan. The options are divided into short- and long-term. Select which you will begin to use immediately and those you will want to pursue in the future.

Short-term Promotional Options

		Today	1 Year	2 Years	Not in Plan
✓	Invitations	*XX*			
✓	Catalogs	*XX*			
___	Brochures				
___	Tear Sheets				
✓	Press Releases -- Newspapers	*XX*			
___	Press Releases -- Magazines				
___	Public Service Announcements -- Television				
___	Public Service Announcements -- Radio				
___	Editorials/Reviews				
___	Posters				

Special Events

		Today	1 Year	2 Years	Not in Plan
✓	Charity Events		*XX*		
___	Open Houses at Your Studio				
___	Demonstrations -- Art Fairs/Public Places				
✓	Lectures -- Colleges/Universities		*XX*		

Long-term Promotional Options

		Today	1 Year	2 Years	Not in Plan
✓	Catalogs		*XX*	*XX*	*XX*
___	Newsletters				
___	Videos				
___	Advertising				
___	Articles for Publication				
✓	Guest Speaker -- Television Shows			*XX*	
✓	Guest Speaker -- Radio Shows			*XX*	
✓	Books on Your Art			*XX*	

Your Own Promotional Ideas

PUBLISHING YOUR WORK

For many artists, the phrase "publishing your art" conjures up images of a formidable task from which emerges prints by well-known artists. Many artists do not realize the ease and profitability of publishing their art. Publishing is not limited strictly to endeavors involving publishing companies, although that is the most desired route. This chapter is provided to dispel the common myths and misunderstandings about publishing fine art and possibly even to set you on the road to producing limited editions of your own.

What Is Publishing Fine Art?

As we mentioned earlier in this book, publishing is often misunderstood. Let us refer to publishing *as **producing a quantity of work based on the multiplication of a piece***. These pieces are not copies but are usually original works unto themselves. This is referred to as producing "limited editions" or a "series" of pieces. Publishing is not limited to just the painter or photographer. Sculptors and other artisans can also publish their work by creating a piece and then cast additional pieces based upon this first piece. The sculptor would then have a limited edition of pieces to display and sell versus the one single piece. Also, the sculptor could create a piece of work from plaster or wax as the mold and reproduce the image.

Posters are often misconstrued to be fine art. This is not correct; they are considered an advertising medium created through offset lithography, used to alert the public to an upcoming event or as decoration. A poster with or without advertising text is by no means fine art. Do not allow yourself to be convinced otherwise. If you are a commercial artist, you may use posters as another product to sell along with your work.

The ideal circumstance for an artist is to become involved in a venture with a publishing company. This is what most artists consider when the term "publishing" is mentioned. Most publishing companies search for artists whose work they can sell. The artist will provide the work, sometimes sharing the cost of production with the publisher, while the publisher produces the editions and uses its established marketing networks to sell the pieces. If you are able to join such a venture, I recommend you do so. Be sure you are being equitably treated by the publisher when it comes down to the final distribution of revenue. Always consult with your attorney before signing any contracts.

Who Can Publish Their Work? When?

Publishing is a viable option for most commercial and fine artists. This is especially beneficial for artists who tend not to be prolific. These artists will find that galleries are not interested in their work because they do not produce enough to support the gallery's efforts, time, energy, and expense to promote. Publishing will allow these artists to create more work within a shorter period of time, thereby broadening the market.

Why Publish Your Work?

There are many advantages to publishing your work, even beyond the potential financial benefits. Granted, earning a living is always a novel idea, but publishing can serve further objectives as well. Providing works in multiples expands your visibility within the art community. This helps accelerate the value of other works as your work becomes more recognizable and accessible before a greater number of collectors. Publishing can make your work more attractive to a gallery by giving them a broader price range in which to sell. As your work becomes more accessible to more galleries, potential opportunities with additional galleries will arise. The benefits of publishing begin to gather their own momentum.

An artist should also consider the size of the original works in relation to what people can hang in their gallery, institution, or home. If you work in large wall pieces, the number of people who can hang such a piece is limited. For example, the Japanese live in very small homes so the art they collect is small in size, proportional with the size of their homes. Now, for the artists who like to work in large pieces, publishing can be a way in which they can produce pieces of a smaller size as a multiple of the larger piece; these are known as "afters." Give thought to how your collectors will use the piece when considering your publishing options.

Some collectors purchase prints rather than paintings, not only for reasons of affordability but also because they believe that selling a print on the secondary market gives them access to a greater number of potential buyers. The print is viewed by these collectors as more of a commodity than is one original work of art. With numerous prints the same as theirs circulating in the art community, there is more visibility of the work, enhancing the collector's chances for success at the time of sale. Prints are regularly sold on a secondary market, therefore the collector has the opportunity to take advantage of the promotion the gallery or publisher has already done.

Types of Publishing

A wide variety of printing methods are available to the artist who wishes to create limited editions. Some common methods include:

Serigraphy	More commonly known as silk screening, serigraphy is a printing process in which the medium (ink, acrylic, etc.) is forced through a fine screen with a squeegee.
Woodcut	Woodcut is a relief printing technique in which the printing surface is carved with special wood-cutting tools. The printing medium is then applied directly to the wood and pressed onto a surface such as paper, fabric, glass, or wood.

Etchings — Etchings are a type of print made by drawing with a steel etching needle or tool on a highly polished plate. As with the woodcut method, the printing media is applied directly to the plate and pressed onto a paper or fabric surface.

Lithography — Lithography is a process in which the printing surface has been sensitized by chemical means. The ink picks up the design of the treated areas and not the blank areas. The ink is then transferred onto the paper or fabric.

Mixed Media — Mixed media combines two or more of the above offering a variation in each print that makes each unique and therefore often more desirable. Mixed media begins with one or more of the above methods finished by painting or working on each individual print to make it unique. Of the methods listed, this is considered the most popular and the best way to start out if you are on a limited budget.

Others — Some artists are quite creative in designing their own printing techniques. In 1989, we held a David Hockney exhibition at the museum. At the opening, Hockney arranged for a facsimile machine to be set up. He pre-programmed the facsimile at his studio to send images of his art to the museum. As he arrived for the exhibition, so did his art over the facsimile machine. The pages were then pinned on the walls in designated areas, becoming the exhibition. It was quite a media extravaganza!

He later stated he was not producing the work to sell, as the facsimile image would fade and has no real value. He was interested in the idea that fine art images could be transferred with this type of technology.

The Cost of Publishing Your Work

The cost of creating limited editions can range greatly, depending on the method you use. If you are working within a modest budget, set your creative talents to the task. One artist I worked with was quite ingenious. She prepared the master plate from a sheet of steel, applied ink to the plate, placed paper on the plate, and then drove her car over the entire contraption. This may not be a conventional method of creating prints, but it was quite effective. I am not advocating using your car as a printing press, but it shows that if you put your creative talents to the task and are willing to experiment a bit, you will find ways to produce good prints.

Local colleges and universities provide classes in print making. Taking one of these classes will give you the opportunity to try out various techniques at little cost. Plus, you may be able to create a small limited edition during the run of the class.

Many books have been written on the subject of printing fine art. Take time to review these books for ideas you can use with your own work. Remember; offset lithography is not a fine art printing process. It is a photomechanical process of printing used for posters, greeting cards, and the like. I recommend avoiding this method for fine art limited editions.

What Artworks Can Be Published?

Almost any piece can be published, but it will be up to you as the artist to decide which is the best to publish. A painter, for example, will want to select a piece that reproduces well. A sculptor may wish to select a piece that is not so large that the cost of multiplying the art may price the edition out of the targeted marketplace.

Always keep your ears and eyes open during your exhibitions. Observe which pieces receive the most attention from collectors, dealers, and others. If the piece you select has been well received by a number of people, that piece probably stands a greater chance of success. Many artists will make the mistake of selecting a sentimental favorite, even if the piece did not seem to stimulate the public. Seek the advice of art professionals you trust.

Once again, artists who work in large pieces will want to consider reducing the physical size of the multiples. How many people can hang the painting of a reclining 6-foot woman over their couch? In contrast, how many people can hang the print of a woman if it were reduced to a 24 x 30 inch size print? Many artists who are print makers share the belief that if an image is reproduced from another existing image, then it is not legitimate. This is something you as the artist have to decide.

What Size Edition Works Best?

It is my opinion that you should begin with low numbers in your edition, anywhere from fifteen to twenty-five. Small editions are generally within the budget and marketing capabilities of the average artist. Small editions do not flood the market with too many pieces, which can drop the value of the works. If you are after the more commercial side of the market, you may consider producing your edition in a series of twos or fours. People often collect pieces in pairs.

When you publish your own work, you have total control over pricing, medium, edition size and so forth. It is important to understand that the word "limited" means just that. It is frowned upon by the art world when edition sizes go much beyond 100 prints; even fewer numbers are acceptable for sculpture editions. Publishers will tend to expand the edition sizes to much larger numbers. In my opinion, editions of 350 to 500 become "unlimited editions." The cost per piece comes down as the size of the edition gets larger, tempting many artists and publishers by the bottom line. Astute collectors often stay away from these works.

Edition size is a decision I think only the artist should make, based upon his or her career plan. If your primary interest is to increase revenues and not about raising the importance of your work, then by all means, go for it.

Marketing Your Prints

Before you actually begin producing your limited edition, give a great deal of thought about how to market them. I have seen many artists go full steam ahead with the creative work -- which I will admit is more interesting -- and completely neglect deciding how they are going to market the final product. The biggest advantage to being involved in a venture with a good publisher is being able to utilize the publisher's marketing network. Before publishers ever begin expending monies on creating limited editions, they will have a complete plan as to which networks and contacts will be used to sell the editions as quickly as possible. You should also think like this.

If you have already developed a mailing list of collectors and potential collectors, start by approaching them with the opportunity to purchase on the front end of the edition. Many galleries also like to offer collectors a discount or a pre-published price, which means you can take orders before the print is completed. This can help defer the cost of printing, etc. It can be a great opportunity for everyone involved.

You have many alternatives for marketing your prints. The most important thing to keep in mind is that once you have produced the quality limited edition, you will need to create a sales and marketing tool to promote the series. This is a good reason to keep the edition size and the costs down.

If you are self publishing your own work in small edition sizes, an easy yet impressive tool for selling a print is a tear sheet, like the example shown on the following page. A relatively inexpensive tear sheet can be made easily using a word processor and a 35mm color print. Following the example, print your own information on the page. Attach the photograph of the work on the upper section of the page, as shown.

If you are working with a publisher, they will usually handle the promotional materials, distribution and so forth. Usually, a large number of tear sheets and informational materials on the artist are prepared. The publisher then mass mails to potential dealers and galleries. If you set publishing as a goal, that is to contract with a publisher, make sure you understand what type of work they sell. This will save you a great deal of time.

JEROME GASTALDI

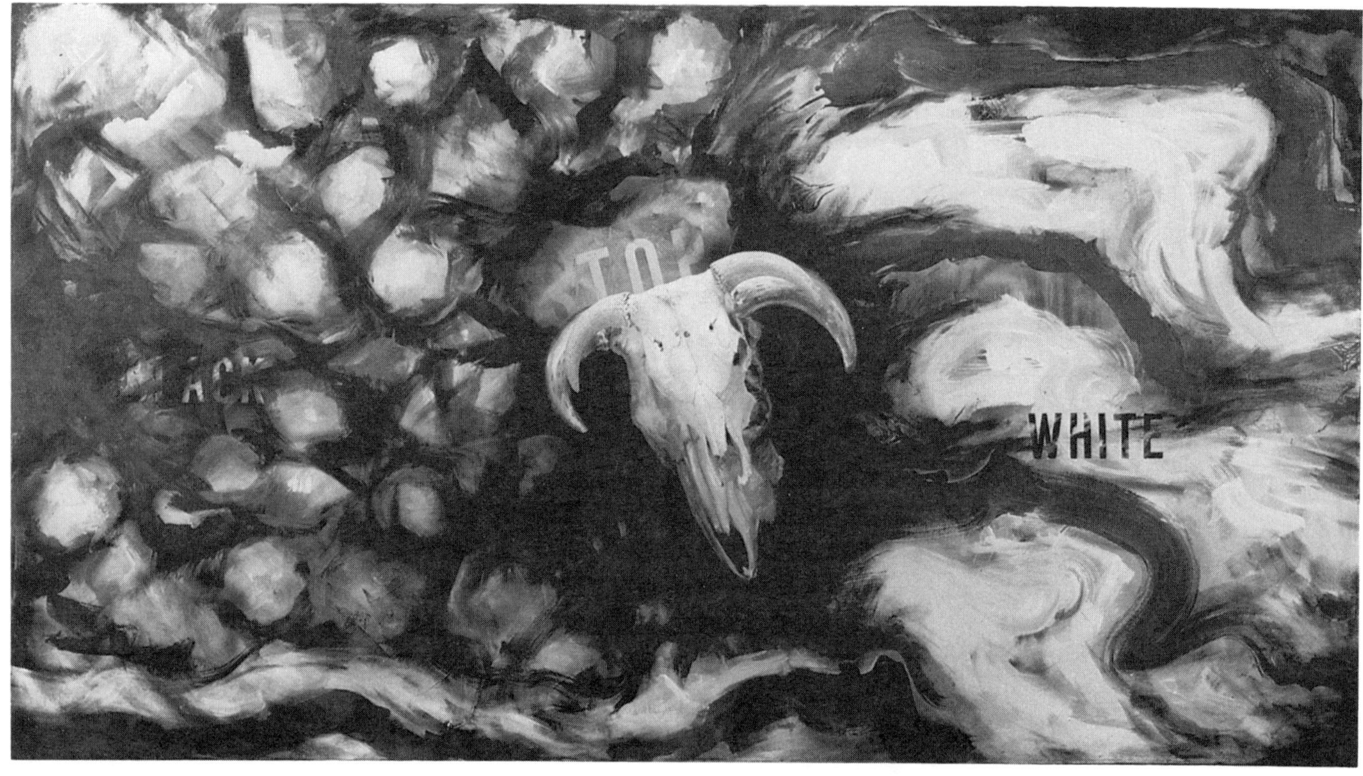

Gastaldi's works deal with the issue that we are subjected to good as well as negative information and we should question the direct as well as the subliminal.

<u>Black and White</u>
Mixed Media
Serigraph, Lithography, and Hand Worked
on 100% Museum Rag
24" x 48"
Total edition limited to 16 numbered prints.
Completion in 1991

CAREER PLAN

Production & Marketing Costs Worksheet

Before you begin spending any money, take the time to research exactly what each phase of the production process will cost you. Use accurate figures when estimating your costs. In cases in which you are using outside resources, it is advisable to obtain at least three bids before settling on a vendor.

Once you have determined the subtotal numbers A, B, C, and D, transpose those numbers to the last page of this worksheet for final calculations and analysis.

Piece(s) Selected for this Limited Edition: ____________________

Method of Production: ____________________ Size of Edition: __________

Raw Material Costs:

	Type of Material	Resource	Qty	Cost/Unit	Total Cost
1.	________	______	___	______	______
2.	________	______	___	______	______
3.	________	______	___	______	______
4.	________	______	___	______	______
5.	________	______	___	______	______
6.	________	______	___	______	______
7.	________	______	___	______	______
8.	________	______	___	______	______
9.	________	______	___	______	______
10.	________	______	___	______	______

(A) Total Raw Material Costs: $ ______

Processing Costs:

	Process Required	Vendor	Bidded Cost
1.	______________	______________	________
2.	______________	______________	________
3.	______________	______________	________
4.	______________	______________	________
	(B) Total Processing Costs:		$ ______

Marketing Costs:

Type of Marketing Tool to Be Produced for your Print Edition: ______________________

No. People Soliciting: __________ Qty. Pieces to Be Produced: ___________

Costs to Producing the Low Cost Tear Sheet:

	Material Required	Resource	Qty	Cost/Unit	Total Cost
1.	Paper	________	__	________	________
2.	Photograph Processing	________	__	________	________
3.	Photograph Duplication	________	__	________	________
4.	Word Processing Fees	________	__	________	________
5.	Photocopying Fees	________	__	________	________
6.	Color Copying Fees	________	__	________	________
7.	Envelopes	________	__	________	________
8.	Postage	________	__	________	________
	(C) Total Marketing Costs:				**$** ______

Marketing Costs (to produce your own list of other marketing materials for your edition.)

	Material Required	Resource	Qty	Cost/Unit	Total Cost
1.	Catalog	________	___	________	________
2.	Brochure	________	___	________	________
3.	Other Tear Sheets	________	___	________	________
4.	________________	________	___	________	________
5.	________________	________	___	________	________
6.	________________	________	___	________	________
7.	________________	________	___	________	________
8.	________________	________	___	________	________
9.	________________	________	___	________	________
10.	________________	________	___	________	________
	(D) Total Custom Marketing Costs:				$ ______

Total Costs of Producing the Limited Edition

(A) Total Raw Material Costs: $ ______

(B) Total Processing Costs: $ ______

(C) Total Marketing Costs: $ ______

or

(D) Total Custom Marketing Costs: $ ______

Total Costs of Production: $ ______

Projected Costs per Unit (Total Costs of Production/Edition Size): $ ______

Is this total expense within your budget guidelines? Yes ___ No ___

Pricing Your Prints

When establishing the pricing structure for your prints, keep in mind that the gallery must make money on the proposition as well. Establish a wholesale price and a retail price for each edition. The retail price - the price paid by the public for the piece - should be at least double the wholesale price - the price the gallery is to pay you for the piece. When you produce smaller numbers within the edition, the dealer should be able to raise the retail price of the piece more rapidly.

It is easy for you to determine the "going rate" for prints by artists who work in a similar style and medium. Look through the various art publications for prints and pricing. You may wish to subscribe to a number of publications to stay in tune with the going market for prints. Check with galleries in your area that exhibit works similar to your own. Get the opinions of respected art professionals whom you trust. Being well informed will help you properly price your works.

Many artists make the mistake of becoming too greedy, thinking the gallery is making all the money. Keep in mind that the gallery has a much larger overhead to carry than does the artist and is supporting the expense of marketing the works as well. The relationship between the artist and the gallery is like a marriage. You have to work together to be successful. Again, choose your gallery representation with care.

It is important when pricing your prints to remember that both you and the gallery must be able to make a reasonable profit. I have seen cases where artists have underpriced their work so dramatically that it has hindered obtaining gallery support for their prints. An artist I worked with published an edition of 100 serigraph prints. He planned to sell the prints at a wholesale price of $30 and at a suggested retail gallery price of $60. Unfortunately, this would not be of interest to most fine art galleries. Even if the gallery sold 50% of the edition, they could only make $1,500. You must think of the needs of your gallery as well as yourself.

Sample Price Schedules

A wholesale/retail price should be established for each limited edition you produce. Samples have been provided on the following page. The goal of a price schedule is to gradually escalate the price of the print as the supply of available prints for sale begins to diminish. As the resource of available stock decreases, the value of the stock increases and the price goes up. This escalation gives an incentive to the collector to purchase up front, when the edition first comes out, rather than to wait until the supply dwindles. If you are working with a publisher, this will most likely be taken care of for you.

In the first example, the limited edition consisted of twenty prints of a moderately priced artist. As the number of prints in the edition were sold, the price began to rise. This allows a record of increased value to be established.

Sample Price Schedule Structures

Edition Size: 20

No. of Prints Sold	No. Left to Sell	Wholesale	Retail
1 to 5 prints	15	$ 150.00	$ 300.00+
6 to 10 prints	10	$ 213.00	$ 426.00+
11 to 15 prints	5	$ 291.00	$ 582.00+
16 to 20 prints	0	$ 400.00	$1000.00+

Edition Size: 100

No. of Prints Sold	No. Left to Sell	Wholesale	Retail
1 to 25 prints	75	$ 450.00	$ 900.00+
26 to 50 prints	50	$ 513.00	$1026.00+
51 to 75 prints	25	$ 591.00	$1182.00+
76 to 100 prints	0	$ 800.00	$1900.00+

CAREER PLAN

Price Schedule Worksheet

Develop a wholesale/retail price schedule for your limited edition series.

What artists create prints of works similar in style, media, and importance to your own?

1. ______________________ 4. ______________________

2. ______________________ 5. ______________________

3. ______________________ 6. ______________________

What price range do their original works sell in?

Your Art: $ ________________

1. $______________________ 4. $______________________

2. $______________________ 5. $______________________

3. $______________________ 6. $______________________

What price range do their prints sell in? (Include research on how the price has varied from when the edition was first released to when the edition was closer to selling out.)

1. $______________________ 4. $______________________

2. $______________________ 5. $______________________

3. $______________________ 6. $______________________

Where are their prints primarily sold? Can you use this same marketing approach for your work? Explain.

1. ______________________ 4. ______________________

2. ______________________ 5. ______________________

3. ______________________ 6. ______________________

Now, create a four-tier schedule based upon the above research with each tier, for example, may consist of 25% of the entire edition. You will find that you may need to draft and redraft this schedule until you feel comfortable with the numbers.

Cost per Unit to Produce: ________ Total Cost of Production: ________

Edition size: _____________ Tier Size (Edition/4): ________________

Tier 1: Prints: _____ to _____ Wholesale: _____ Suggested Retail: _____ to _____
Tier 2: Prints: _____ to _____ Wholesale: _____ Suggested Retail: _____ to _____
Tier 3: Prints: _____ to _____ Wholesale: _____ Suggested Retail: _____ to _____
Tier 4: Prints: _____ to _____ Wholesale: _____ Suggested Retail: _____ to _____

Wholesale Revenue = No. of prints in tier x wholesale price

WR earned if Tier 1 sold out: ________ x ________ = __________
WR earned if Tier 2 sold out: ________ x ________ = __________
WR earned if Tier 3 sold out: ________ x ________ = __________
WR earned if Tier 4 sold out: ________ x ________ = __________

Total WR earned from sale of the entire edition: $_________

Total Projected Production & Marketing Costs: $_________

Net Profit = WR earned - Total Costs: Tier 1 $_________

Tier 2 $_________

Tier 3 $_________

Tier 4 $_________

Projected Total Net Profits: $_________

When do you expect to reach the break-even point (cost=sales)?

Tier 1: ___ (25%) Tier 2: ___ (50%) Tier 3: ___ (75%) Tier 4: ___ (100%)

Is this break-even and profit potential acceptable to you? Yes ____ No ____
(If No, rework your sales schedule, reviewing sale prices and costs of production.)

** ***Artist proofs are not included in the above calculations. The Artist Proofs can total approximately 10% of the edition.***

An Experience in Self-Publishing

In March of 1991, the opportunity arose for me to publish a print that could be offered at a show of my work scheduled for June. My dealer thought it would be a good idea to have this print available because we could offer something in a very affordable price range, thereby developing a broader range of collectors. Knowing that I was an unknown artist at the time, I felt it was unlikely that any publisher would take a chance on my works. I decided to publish the print myself.

The decision was made to produce a mixed-media serigraph with a certain amount of handwork on each piece. An edition of sixteen pieces without proofs was printed. It was difficult at first to interest a printer in this job. The quantity to be printed was smaller than what most printers are interested in doing because they cannot make the money they would with a larger project. The cost of each print was much higher per unit than for a larger edition. I found a small print studio that agreed to do the print with me.

I worked with the printer on every aspect of the piece; design, color, pulling of each pass of the squeegee. I finished each print with a fair amount of handwork. The prints turned out quite good. In retrospect, my main mistake was that this edition was too small. I had not fully evaluated the complete costs. I could have completed an edition twice the size for about the same cost and still stayed within my budget and still have kept it within a reasonable edition size.

This limited edition was still a good thing to do even though it was not as profitable a venture as it could have been. It opened up the opportunity to do a much larger edition a few months later. The owners of a fine art publication purchased one of the first prints and as a result approached me with a proposal to use one of my images on the cover of their publication if I would do a new edition. They also offered to market the first 25% of my next edition through their distribution network. I took them up on their offer.

Knowing the costs I had just undertaken previously, I did not want to chance funding a larger edition on my own. I approached a printer with a proposal to joint-venture the edition with me. We split the costs and the ownership of the edition. It provided me the opportunity to have another edition out there and provided the printer the opportunity to share in the revenues. The printer was already set up with proper shipping and storage facilities; something I did not want to invest in at the time. It's important to look at the print not only as a potential money maker but also as free advertising.

Finding and Landing a Publisher

Landing a contract with a reputable publisher requires the same tenacity as obtaining representation in a gallery or institution. You want to know the publisher is capable of producing and selling your editions, will have concern regarding the manner in which they market the editions and will be fair and equitable in the distribution of profits from the sales of your art.

This is where qualifying the publisher is imperative. Who have they published? How does your work relate to the publisher's focus? When you feel you have found a suitable publisher, use the presentation materials and methods you have developed in the earlier chapters to introduce yourself to the publisher. The same rules of presentation apply to the publisher as to any other venue. Never send out a package to an unsolicited target.

The primary goal in publishing your art is to encourage people to see and buy your art work. Associating yourself with a reputable publisher increases your chances for success in contrast to trying to market a limited edition alone. If you present your work to a qualified publisher, the publisher will more likely be able to see your marketability within their network.

Each publisher will have advantages and disadvantages in relation to the goals you have set for yourself. One publisher may be perfect in giving you the exposure and recognition you need to lead you to more prominent exposure. Consider all the options. Publishers have their own set of goals. They have a specific focus that they pursue. In the process of qualifying contacts, you will learn about their focus, saving you time, money and frustration.

Select your publishers with care. Some are more businesslike than others. Recently, an artist who came to me for consultation had just come from an unfortunate experience with a publisher. In fact, at the time we spoke, she was in court trying to obtain the royalty fees due her. She had signed a contract that allowed the publisher to purchase and publish her work. As compensation, she was to receive continuous royalties from the sales.

Her work was well received as the publisher sold nearly $1 million of her prints. Unfortunately, the company declared bankruptcy, absconding with her royalty fees. The company further chose to "dump" their remaining inventory on the market, resulting in an instant crash of the value of her limited edition pieces. You must be very careful in selecting your publisher, as publishers can do an equal amount of damage to your reputation and financial health as they can benefit it.

Be wary of publishers who approach you to promote your work with exclusive contracts or promises of mass printing. It sounds good up front, but be careful. Before signing any contracts, have a lawyer look over the paper work. Make sure a performance/cancellation clause beneficial to you is included within the contract. Before signing, have all your questions answered, and be clear on what you are getting involved in.

Teleresearch Worksheet: Publishers

Date of Contact: *04 / 22 / 93*

Source of Listing: *Anderson*
Referred by: *Anderson*
Goal of this call:
✓ Research Information
✓ Solicit Interest
__ Land Contract

Name of Publisher: *The Chicago Fine Art Publishers, Inc.*
Address: *770 N. Michigan Ave.*
____
City: *Chicago*
State: *IL* Zip: *60611* Country: *USA*
Telephone: *(312) 337-5501* Facsimile: *(312) 337-0000*

Owner/Decision Maker: *Albert Greer* Title: *Director*
Spoke With: *William Greer* Position/Title: *Sr. Manager*

What type of publisher is this?
✓ Fine Art
✓ Limited Editions
__ Posters
✓ Books
__ Commercial Art
__ Unlimited Editions
__ Secondary Products
__ Other: ________

What types of art do they publish? *Contemporary Art*
What is the publisher's focus/goals? *Emerging Contemporary Artists*

What type of publishing methods do they use?
✓ Serigraphy
✓ Etchings
✓ Mixed Media
__ Woodcut
__ Lithography
__ Offset Litho **

***** Remember -- Offset lithography is not a fine art publishing technique. Are they representing this method as a fine art technique? If so, they may not be as experienced as they represent.***

Are the original works limited to a specific price range? *$ 500.00* to *$ 5,000.00*
Are the editions limited to a specific price range? *$ 100.00* to *$ 1,000.00*

Is my work appropriate for this publisher? ✓ Yes __ No (Ask for a referral)

Whom do they currently represent? *They have published well over 30 artists, some of whom I have heard of. Others whom I have not. They are willing to take a risk on new artists they feel they can promote and sell.*
__ Blue Chip Artists ✓ New Artists

Do they take on new artists? ✓ Yes __ No (Ask for a referral)

What are their presentation policies? *Submit printed materials of the work including any prints which have been done before for the quality of work, etc. Include catalog of work. Not just slides.*

Who should the materials be directed to? *William Greer*

How long have they been publishing? *15 years*
Do they do any other businesses, too? __ Yes ✓ No
Are they financially sound? *Yes. They have done well with the artists they have selected. They have not expanded beyond what their artists can support.*

Any Better Business Bureau Reports against them? __ Yes ✓ No
Any credit recordings in their county against them? __ Yes ✓ No

How do they market their published works?

✓ direct contacts	✓ expositions	__ stores
✓ galleries	✓ catalogs	__ brochures
__ fliers	__ posters	__ literature
__ other ______		

Are they represented at art expos or important art events? ✓ Yes __ No
Do they have a reputation for building careers? ✓ Yes __ No
Sales? ✓ Yes __ No

What is their standard program for working with an artist?
They pay the artist a percentage for producing the print and a royalty from each print sold.

What are their standard revenue distribution policies?
Royalty payments are distributed quarterly based on gross sales.

Is the artist bound by an exclusive representation contract? __ Yes ✓ No

***Questions to direct to other artist(s) this publisher represents*:**

What kind of reputation does this publisher have? ______

Do they promptly pay their artists? ______

Have they had any difficulties dealing with the publisher? ______

Referred by this publisher to another: ______________________________

____

Comments: ______________________________

____

____

____

____

____

____

____

Next Step: __ Appointment to present to: ______________________________
Date: ____________ Time: ______ Location: ________

✓ Mail presentation materials to: *William Greer*

__ Call again at a future date (schedule it in your calendar)
Ask for: ______________________________

__ Not a viable publisher

PRICING YOUR WORK

Pricing your works is the same for originals as it is for limited editions. It requires thorough research of the marketplaces you are targeting and the artists who are already selling there. Remember to compare apples to apples and oranges to oranges. Look at the successes of the artists who are similar in style, medium, and importance to yourself. There is no sense blowing your perceptions out of proportion by following a blue chip artist's sales record, unless that is where you are or intend to be. For now, research artists who are similar to yourself.

How do you find this information? You can begin by using the various art publications to identify the artists you want to investigate. Use your Artist Research Worksheet to ask the key questions that will help you identify the artists' backgrounds, importance, and pricing for their works.

You may need to visit some of the venues in person. Ask for materials about the artists and a price sheet for the gallery. Talk with the representative who is there. He or she may provide information regarding the pricing of other comparative artists. People love to give opinions and show their range of knowledge about art and artists. If you are preparing for your first show, you may wish to price your work by comparing your work aesthetically to other available works. Additionally, take into consideration your financial needs.

Developing a Pricing Structure

Armed with the information you have researched, you are ready to price your own work. The first step if you have had prior sales is to look at the prices you have received in the past. What were the prices? Did you meet with resistance with these prices? By whom? Is this the person to whom you are marketing your work to now? If not, do not be overly concerned with his or her objections at this time.

Using the Sales Evaluation Worksheet, list all the pieces you have sold in the past, the offering price, and the actual price you received for the piece. Note how the pieces were sold whether it be directly from your studio, through a representative, gallery or whom ever. Has the price of your work increased, decreased, or remained the same over time? Look at all this information.

Now look at what comparable artist's works are selling for. How do their pieces compare to yours? Set your prices based on all this information. Listen to the suggestions given by your gallery or dealer as to what they feel your work should sell for. Remember that you should make the final decisions, being realistic as to what you can reasonably expect.

Be Consistent with Your Prices

If you are offering a piece through your gallery at one price, maintain that price if you are also offering it outside the gallery. The quickest way to lose gallery representation and greatly diminish your chances for future representation is to undercut the gallery's efforts. You are supposed to work with your representation, not compete with it.

Further, if you are represented by numerous galleries in numerous cities, keep your pricing consistent between the galleries. Offer your work to each gallery at similar prices. The dealers may talk to each other and, if you charge one dealer a significantly greater price for a piece than another, you will damage your relationship with both. One will view you as biased, the other will view you as dishonest. Be wary of your business reputation.

I live in a Southern California art community. Through the years I have become friends with many artists, dealers, and gallery owners. I can assure you it is public information who will "back door" works from their studio to make a sale or adjust (generally lower) the price the art is receiving. The dealers do not want to deal with artists that will sabotage the efforts of their gallery.

Don't Be Greedy, But Don't Undervalue Yourself Either

I found it helpful for my own art work to have someone whose judgment I trust look over my prices. This person can help avoid over- or under-valuing the work. I have seen numerous artists grossly inflate the value of their works after having earned a bit of success. It is important not to become a legend in your own mind. Once you have established high prices you do not want to drop them; that can be perceived as a negative. Also, the higher the prices, the smaller the market and the fewer collectors. I always urge artists to be somewhat conservative with the inflation of their prices. A good dealer will help you.

You can raise the price of your works after having successes, such as being included in an important collection, picked up by a prestigious gallery, exhibited by museums, or selected for the collection of a museum. That is how you raise the value of your work. Take it step by step. You may find that a market was receptive to your work at one price for the current time, but if you dramatically raise the price, you may put yourself out of that market. My advice to the artist is to use discretion and not be greedy. The law of supply and demand applies.

In regards to greed, numerous artists will become disgruntled with their gallery as they see the gallery taking a large cut from the revenues of a sale. Keep in mind that the gallery has a larger overhead than you do. It is supporting the cost of displaying and marketing the works. The gallery needs to make as fair a profit in the sale as do you. Traditionally, a fifty-fifty split is accepted.

On the other hand, do not undervalue your work either. Collectors will wonder what is wrong with the work if the artist does not value it highly. Keep in mind who your buyers are and what they are willing to pay. Keep a habit of knowing what the fair market value is for your work and that of similar artists.

Keep an Accurate Record of Your Sales

It is imperative for you to keep a current and accurate record of the sales of all your works. You will be able to discern any trends occurring with your work such as rises and falls in perceived value, paid prices, who is collecting your work, and who is not. You will be able to see whether a venue has any trends to it such as you would experience, for example, in a vacation town with a high tourist trade during certain times of year. Knowledge is power -- the power for you to get the most from your work.

Artist Research Worksheet

Date of Contact: _03 / 24 / 93_ Source of Listing: _Hillsing_
Referred by: _M. Hillsing_

Name of Artist: _Jerry Freeman_
Represented By: _Anne Gallant_
Address: _1342 Bluebird Canyon Drive_
City: _Los Angeles_
State: _CA_ Zip: _90046_ Country: _USA_
Telephone: _(714) 555-3300_ Facsimile: ____________

Birthplace of the Artist: _Oakland, CA_ Year of Birth: _1945_

Type of Art -- Describe the art (subject matter, media, dimensions, prolificacy, etc.): _Contemporary Artist - Paints abstract, generally large. Likes to use acrylics over oils. Paintings range from 3' x 3' to 8' x 10'. Subject matter tends to be about social issues, especially abuse of the young in our society. Colors tend to be dark, somber. Prolificacy - produces 2 paintins a week, very loose style which allows him to work fast. Sells work unframed._

If you can, obtain a copy of the artist's biography sheet as this will provide a great deal of the following information.

Years as an Artist?: _15 yrs._ __ Blue Chip Artist ✓ New Artist

Education?: _Self taught artist. BS - UC Berkley, 1968, Microbiology._

Biography of Exhibitions: _(biography attached)_
✓ Local ✓ Regional __ National __ International

What is the artist's prominence within the art community?: Fairly established So. Cal. area.

Is a catalog of current works available?: ✓ Yes __ No

Is there a price list of current works available?: ✓ Yes (Ask for one to be sent to you.) __ No

How long has the artist been represented by this dealer?: _1 year_

What is the prominence of this dealer in the art community?: _25 years dealer_

What other dealers represent this artist? : _None_

What other artists are represented along with this artist? _Victoria Newman, Justin Resnick_

Sales Evaluation Worksheet

This worksheet is for you to organize chronologically prior sales of your works. It is important for you to have a clear picture of what has been accomplished to date and how. You will see trends over time among venues either good or bad once you have organized the information properly.

Sale Date	Title	List Price	Sold For	Difference	By Whom	Type
______	________	$ ______	$ ______	$ ______	________	D/G/I
______	________	$ ______	$ ______	$ ______	________	D/G/I
______	________	$ ______	$ ______	$ ______	________	D/G/I
______	________	$ ______	$ ______	$ ______	________	D/G/I
______	________	$ ______	$ ______	$ ______	________	D/G/I
______	________	$ ______	$ ______	$ ______	________	D/G/I
______	________	$ ______	$ ______	$ ______	________	D/G/I
______	________	$ ______	$ ______	$ ______	________	D/G/I
______	________	$ ______	$ ______	$ ______	________	D/G/I
______	________	$ ______	$ ______	$ ______	________	D/G/I
______	________	$ ______	$ ______	$ ______	________	D/G/I
______	________	$ ______	$ ______	$ ______	________	D/G/I
______	________	$ ______	$ ______	$ ______	________	D/G/I
______	________	$ ______	$ ______	$ ______	________	D/G/I
______	________	$ ______	$ ______	$ ______	________	D/G/I
______	________	$ ______	$ ______	$ ______	________	D/G/I
______	________	$ ______	$ ______	$ ______	________	D/G/I
______	________	$ ______	$ ______	$ ______	________	D/G/I
______	________	$ ______	$ ______	$ ______	________	D/G/I

D: Dealer G: Gallery I: Independent Dealer

Sales Record

Keeping sales records is imperative for any business, including that of being a professional artist. This is not only for your proper tax reporting records, but for your own market research on what has been successful and what markets may be providing revenue that you had not even thought of focusing on. Work with your data to see trends in your sales.

Title of Piece: ______________________________ Date of Sale: __________

Sold By: ________________________________ Venue Type: G/D/I
Contact Name: ____________________________ Time Listed: __________
Address: ____
City: __________________ State:____ Zip:________
Telephone: ______________ Facsimile: ______________

Sold To: __________________________________ Collector Type: __________
Address: ____
City: __________________ State:____ Zip:________
Telephone: ______________ Facsimile: ______________

Listed Price: $ __________ Sold For: $ ______________
Net Monies Received: $ __________ Monies Paid Venue: $ ______________

Title of Piece: ______________________________ Date of Sale: __________

Sold By: ________________________________ Venue Type: G/D/I
Contact Name: ____________________________ Time Listed: __________
Address: ____
City: __________________ State:____ Zip:________
Telephone: ______________ Facsimile: ______________

Sold To: __________________________________ Collector Type: __________
Address: ____
City: __________________ State:____ Zip:________
Telephone: ______________ Facsimile: ______________

Listed Price: $ __________ Sold For: $ ______________
Net Monies Received: $ __________ Monies Paid Venue: $ ______________

Sales Record

Title of Piece: ______________________ Date of Sale: __________

Sold By: ______________________ Venue Type: G/D/I
Contact Name: ______________________ Time Listed: __________
Address: ______________________
City: ______________ State:____ Zip:________
Telephone: ______________ Facsimile: ______________

Sold To: ______________________ Collector Type: __________
Address: ______________________
City: ______________ State:____ Zip:________
Telephone: ______________ Facsimile: ______________

Listed Price: $ __________ Sold For: $ ______________
Net Monies Received: $ __________ Monies Paid Venue: $ ______________

Title of Piece: ______________________ Date of Sale: __________

Sold By: ______________________ Venue Type: G/D/I
Contact Name: ______________________ Time Listed: __________
Address: ______________________
City: ______________ State:____ Zip:________
Telephone: ______________ Facsimile: ______________

Sold To: ______________________ Collector Type: __________
Address: ______________________
City: ______________ State:____ Zip:________
Telephone: ______________ Facsimile: ______________

Listed Price: $ __________ Sold For: $ ______________
Net Monies Received: $ __________ Monies Paid Venue: $ ______________

FINDING FUNDING FOR YOUR WORK

As part of developing your career plan, consider the supportive opportunities made available to artists through grants, artist-in-residency programs and sponsorships. Grants and programs for the visual artists are available for all types of work and all types of artists. These programs can be used to obtain financial support and time to develop your work and career. Both you and the sponsoring organization benefit from these opportunities.

What is a Grant?

A grant is an award of cash or provision of materials based upon a given set of criteria. These criteria are determined by the sponsoring organization and are based upon the focus of the organization's efforts. For example, one artist I work with obtained funding to develop a traveling exhibition of works based upon art created by the institutionalized insane. For the artist, it was an opportunity to support an issue he felt strongly about and to be financially supported for the efforts. For the sponsoring organization, it was an opportunity to educate the public about this social issue. Both parties benefitted.

What is an Artist-in-Residency Program?

An artist-in-residency program is a form of grant designed to provide artists with the opportunity to live and work in an environment conducive to artistic development. The artist may be given a place to live, work and exhibit over a prescribed length of time. Funds include financial support to the artist during the time of residency. On occasion, part of the residency program will involve teaching or lecturing on the part of the artist.

What are Sponsorships?

Sponsorships are projects funded by individuals, organizations and corporations, again usually based upon the focus of their efforts or products. For example, an artist who works with photography may obtain a sponsorship from a company whose focus is photographic materials or processing. The opportunities for these kinds of sponsorships are endless.

Who Qualifies?

You do! Once again, the qualifications for a grant are established by the sponsoring organization and may include things such as birthplace, heritage, experience, age, sex, style of art, subject matter, project, religious affiliation, financial need, etc. There are grants based upon just about anything you can think of and then some. It will be your job to search through the grant resources to find those which interest you.

Many artists are intimidated by the idea of applying for grants. They are overwhelmed by the prospect of filling out applications, submitting materials and possibly even being interviewed. You need not be. The techniques for presenting to potential venues which you have learned and put into practice through this book apply just the same when approaching for grants.

How Are Grants Awarded?

The actual process is determined by the sponsoring organization but often follows this routine. The artist submits the application along with their presentation materials. These materials are preliminarily reviewed by a selected jury of individuals from the sponsoring organization and/or the community. The preliminary finalists are then selected. Usually a number of reviews take place. The artist may be asked to present works in person or be interviewed by the jury. The award is then presented to the winner or winners.

How Do You Apply For a Grant?

The entire process of applying for a grant is no different than what you do each day in advancing your career.

Grant Research - a.k.a. Market Research

The first step is to investigate what grant opportunities are available to you specifically. Read through the various grant resource books which you can find at bookstores, university, college or public libraries. Identify those grants whose criteria you match. Do not spend the time to apply for a grant if you do not qualify. A number of grant resource listings have been provided in the appendix of this guide.

Investigate the Selected Grants

Begin researching each of the specific grants you have selected. Call or write for the application forms and any additional information which the organization can provide about the grant or itself. The more you know and understand the funding group, the more clearly and focused a presentation you will be able to make. You may even go so far as to ask for a list of the artists who have been awarded the grant in the past including any visual or contact materials they may be able to provide. Grant Research Worksheets have been provided to help you investigate the grant as fully as possible. Be sure to note the grant application deadline.

Develop Your Concept and Proposal

After you have read all the materials collected and before you begin filling out the grant forms, develop a proposal or focus for your presentation. Depending upon the criteria of the grant, develop a concept of how your art will be used or developed in conjunction with their award. For example, if this were a grant involving an environmental issue, how will your art enhance the awareness of this issue to the public? Will it inform the public? Will it be used to intensify emotions or awareness? What are your ideas for this "marriage" of resources?

Unless otherwise instructed by the grant application, this "proposal" is for you to use to focus your answers on the application. If you have a directed goal, your application will reflect that. But conversely, if you are indecisive and do not clearly present your concept to the organization, this too will be obvious.

Completing the Grant Application

For many artists, this is the hardest part of applying for the grant. But now that you understand the grant, the organization and your concept for this project, completing the application will be much easier. Be sure that all your writings are academic in style and not esoteric. Simple, concise and direct responses are far more effective than rambling or flowery answers.

Start by making a few copies of the application which you will use for rough drafts. Keep the original forms aside so they do not become soiled. Read the application thoroughly before answering any questions. Then go back to the beginning and answer each and every question asked on the form. You may wish to use the same kind of language which was used by the organization in its own promotional materials. The terminology an organization uses to describe itself gives the reader a great deal of information.

When this rough draft of the application is completed including any essay writing, have it read over by someone, preferably someone who has an understanding of art, the art community and the focus of this grant. You will find yourself editing the drafts a few times until you feel confident in what you have written.

Once all writing has been finalized, type or laser print the answers onto the original application forms. At no time should a grant application be handwritten. It is important for you to present yourself in an academic fashion just as you would with any presentation. Proof the final application for typos or errors. Make all needed corrections. Make a photocopy of the final application for your own records.

Submit the cover letter, application forms and presentation package to the organization as stated in the instructions. Use a clean, padded presentation style envelope to submit your package. Remember, as always, to clearly label the package and confirm adequate postage.

Follow-up

Stay in contact with the grant committee if possible or the organization which is sponsoring the grant. Call the organization to confirm receipt of your package. When the various key dates of the selection process come up, contact the group for information to determine if you have been selected as a finalist. Remember, though, do not be pushy.

Other Opportunities

There are a wide variety of opportunities you can obtain as an artist for funding your work, above and beyond grants, residency programs and sponsorships. You will find a number of them listed in the grant and residency resource books, but even beyond that, use your imagination. For example, many non-profit organizations look for artists who can help them develop community projects. One artist I work with also produces videos. She used her talents to produce a 15-minute production for the benefit of a struggling non-profit group. The funding for the materials and her time were donated by a benefactor to the organization. She now has an impressive film as part of her portfolio and the non-profit has raised $500,000 for a new building. Again, both parties benefitted.

Your only limitations are your expectations.

Teleresearch Worksheet: Funding Opportunities

Date of Contact: ___________

Source of Listing: _________
Referred by: _____________

Name of Funding: ____
Name of Sponsoring Organization : ________________________________
Address: ____
____
City: ____
State: ______________ Zip: ________ Country: ______________________
Telephone: ________________________ Facsimile: ______________________

Owner/Director: ____________________________ Title: ______________
Spoke with: _______________________________ Position/Title: __________

Date Funding Application is Due: ___________

What type of funding is this?

__ Grant
__ Artist-in-Residency
__ Sponsorship
__ Other ________________________________

What are the funding criteria?

____
____
____

Do you meet all the required criteria? __ Yes __ No

If "No", should you still pursue applying for this award? __ Yes __ No

What is the amount of the award: $________

What other items are awarded? (housing, studio, exhibition space, teaching, etc.)

____
____
____

What are the terms of the award?

____
____
____

What materials are requested to be presented and how?

______

______

______

______

______

______

What is the purpose of the award?

______

______

______

What is the focus of the sponsoring organization?

______

______

______

What are your feelings about their focus, beliefs, products or activities?

______

______

______

Name the artists who received the funding in prior years.

______

______

______

______

______

______

You may wish to call the artists who have been awarded the grant in prior years to ask questions about the organization, application process, their successful presentation, etc.

Comments:

______

______

______

______

______

______

Application Tracking Worksheet

Name of Funding: ____
Name of Sponsoring Organization : ______________________________
Telephone: ____________________

Application Due: __________
Application Submitted: __________
Confirmation of Receipt: __________

Appointment for Presentation: __________
Appointment for Interview: __________

1st Review Cut: ____________________
2nd Review Cut: ____________________
3rd Review Cut: ____________________
4th Review Cut: ____________________
Final Decision: ____________________

Final outcome:

____

____

____

____

Notes and images from application (Remember to retain a copy of the completed application for your records):

APPENDIX

The following references and organizations will help you research information and opportunities to build your career.

Art Law/Accounting

These references and organizations will help you understand your legal and financial responsibilities as a professional artist. For example, in working with contracts, it is important for you to have proper legal advise so that you are properly protected and fully understand what you are obligating yourself to.

American Council for the Arts
1 East 53rd St.
New York, NY 10022

The Artists Friendly Legal Guide
by F. Conner, R. Gilcrest,
P. Karlen, J. Perwin & D. Spatt
Cincinnati: North Light Books
1507 Dana Ave.
Cincinnati, OH 45207
revised: 1988

The Business of Art
by Lee Caplin
New York: Prentice Hall
revised 1991

Legal Guide for the Visual Artist
by Tad Crawford
New York: Allworth Press
revised: 1989

Artists for Tax Equity
Graphic Artists Guild
11 West 20th St., 8th Floor
New York, NY 10011

Business and Legal Forms for Fine Artists
by Tad Crawford
New York: Allworth Press
revised: 1990

The Business of Being an Artist
by Daniel Grant
New York: Allworth Press and
the American Council for the Arts

Volunteer Lawyers for the Arts
1285 Avenue of the Americas
New York, NY 10019

Art Organizations

The purpose of art organizations is to support their artists and enhance the awareness of the arts to the community. The following organizations will serve as starting points for your research. You will find there are additional groups in your local and regional area which may also interest you.

American Association of Museums
1055 thomas Jefferson St., NW
Washington, DC 20007

American Council for the Arts
1285 Avenue of the Americas, 3rd Floor
New York, NY 10019

American Craft Council (ACC)
Division of Continuing Education
604 Goodell Building
University of Massachusetts
Amherst, MA 01003

Artist Equity Association
P.O. Box 28068
Central Station
Washington, DC 20038

Association of Independent Film and Video Makers
625 Broadway, 9th Floor
New York, NY 10003

Artists Consortium Library
1 East 53rd St.
New York, NY 10022

Deaf Artists of America
P.O. Box 18190
Rochester, NY 10003

The Foundation Center
79 5th Ave.
New York, NY 10003

Graphic Artists Guild
11 West 20th St.
New York, NY 10011

National Alliance of Media Arts Centers (NAMAC)
1212 Broadway, Suite 816
Oakland, CA 94612

National Assembly of Local Art Agencies (NALAA)
1420 K St., NW, Suite 204
Washington, DC 20005

National Assembly of State Agencies (NASAA)
1010 Vermont Ave., NW, Suite 920
Washington, DC 20005

National Association of Artists Organizations (NAAO)
1100 Pennsylvania Ave., NW
Washington, DC 20506

National Center on the Arts and Aging
National Council on the Aging
409 3rd St., SW, Suite 200
Washington, DC 20024

National Endowment for the Arts (NEA)
1100 Pennsylvania Ave., NW
Washington, DC 20506

Visual AIDS
131 W. 24th St., 3rd Floor
New York, NY 10011

The Woman's Building
1643 18th St.
Santa Monica, CA 90404

Copyright Registration

Copyrighting your work and the presentation materials, such as catalogs and brochures, is an important aspect of being a professional artist. You put a great deal of effort into your works and it is in your best interest to protect them. The following guides will help you protect your works.

Copyright Information Kit
Copyright Office
Library of Congress
Washington, D.C. 20559

How to Protect Your Creative Work
by David A. Weinstein, John Wiley and Sons
605 Third Ave.
New York, NY 10158

VLA Guide to Copyright for the Visual Arts
Volunteer Lawyers of the Arts
1 East 53rd St.
New York, NY 10022

Employment and Career Opportunities

There are many organizations and publications whose purpose is to help the artist find employment and career opportunities within the arts. They stay on top of what is happening in the local, regional, or national areas.

Art Calendar
P.O. Box 1040
Great Falls, VA 22066

AVISO
American Association of Museums
1225 I St., NW, Suite 200
Washington, D.C. 20005

Arts in Education Program
Office of Public Partnership
National Endowment for the Arts
1100 Pennsylvania Ave., NW
Washington, DC 20506

For the Working Artist: A Survival Guide
by Judith Luther
National Network for Artist Placement
935 W. Avenue 37
Los Angeles, CA 90065

National Art Education Assoc. (NAEA)
1916 Association Dr.
Reston, VA 22091

National Arts Jobbank
236 Montezuma Ave.
Santa Fe, NM 87501

National Directory of Arts Internships
by Warren Christensen
National Network for Artist Placement
935 West Avenue 37
Los Angeles, CA 90065

National Guild of Community Schools of the Arts (NGCSA)
P.O. Box 8018
Englewood, NJ 07631

Fine Art Printing

Finding the right publisher is as important as finding the right dealer representation for your work. The following guide will start you off in the right track.

Directory of Art Publishers, Book Publishers and Record Companies
Directors Guild Publishers and The Consultant Press
P.O. Box 369
Renaissance, CA 95962

Gallery Directories/Dealers

Targeting the right galleries and dealers for your work is an important part of developing your career. Qualifying the venue before you present will save you time, money and frustration. The following organizations and publications will help you begin your search.

American Art Directory
by R.R. Bowker
New York, NY

Art & Auction International Directory
Art & Auction
250 West 57th St.
New York, NY 10107

Art Diary: The World's Art Directory
Milan, Italy: Giancardo Politi Editore
Flash Art
799 Broadway
New York, NY 10003

Directory of Galleries for the Fine Artist
Directors Guild Publishers and
The Consultant Press
P.O. Box 369
Renaissance, CA 95962

International Directory of the Arts
Wittborn Art Books, Inc.
1018 Madison Ave.
New York, NY 10021

American Art Galleries:
The Illustrated Guide to Their Art & Artists
Facts on File
460 Park Ave., South
New York, NY 10016

Art in America Annual Guide
to Galleries, Museums and Artists
Art in America
575 Broadway
New York, NY 10012

Directory of Fine Art Representatives
and Corporate Art Collections
Directors Guild Publishers and
The Consultant Press
P.O. Box 369
Renaissance, CA 95962

Intl. Directory of Corp. Art Collections
ARTnews and International Art Alliance
New York, NY
revised: 1989

The Visual Arts Handbook
Visual Arts Ontario
439 Wellington St.
Toronto, Ontario, Canada M5V 1E7

Grant and Funding Opportunities

Grants and programs for the visual artists are available for all types of work and all types of artists. These programs can be used to obtain financial support and time to develop your work and career. The following organizations and publications will help you begin your research.

Artist Help: The Artist's Guide to Work-related Human & Social Services
by the Research Center for Arts & Culture
Columbia University
Neal-Schuman Publishers
23 Leonard St.
New York, NY 10013
1990

Artist-in-Residency Programs
by Caroll Michels
New York, NY

Directory of Financial Aid for Women
Reference Service Press
1100 Industrial Rd., Suite 9
San Carlos, CA 94070

Directory of Grants in the Humanities
The Onyx Press
4041 N. Central, Suite 700
Phoenix, AZ 85012

Foundation Grants to Individuals
The Foundation Center
79 Fifth Ave.
New York, NY 10003
Revised: 1991

Guide to Programs and Program Application Guidelines and Forms
Public Information Office
National Endowment for the Arts
1100 Pennsylvania Ave., NW
Washington, DC 20506

Money to Work II - Funding for the Visual Artist
Art Resources International with support from the NEA
Edited by Helen M. Brunner, and Donald H. Russell with Grant E. Samuelsen
5813 Nevada Ave., NW
Washington, DC 20015

Money for Visual Artists
by The American Council for the Arts
Edited by: Susanne Niemeyer
New York: Allworth Press

The National Directory of Grants and Aid to Individuals in the Arts
by Nancy A. Fandel
Washington International Arts Letter, 1987
Washington, DC

The Proposal Writer's Guide
by Michael Burns
Development & Technical Assistance Cntr
70 Audubon St.
New Haven, CT 06510

Visual Arts Residency: Sponsor Organizations
Mid-Atlantic Arts Foundation
11 E. Chase St., Suite 2A
Baltimore, MD 21202

Magazines

Subscribe to a number of art publications. These publications will help you stay on top of what is happening in the art world and what venues may be potential candidates for your work. Select a few of the national or international publications, but don't forget to include those that report on the events and artists of your region and style. The following is an introductory list of publications.

American Artist
P.O. Box 1213
Newark, NJ 07101

American Association of Museums
1225 Eye St., NW, #200
Washington, D.C. 20005

Art & Antiques
89 Fifth Ave.
New York, NY 10003

Art & Artists
280 Broadway St., #412
New York, NY 10007

Art & Auction
250 W. 57th St.
New York, NY 10107

Art Beat
P.O. Box 123
Mt. Shasta, CA 96067

Art Business News
P.O. Box 3837
Stamford, CT 06905

Art Gallery International
P.O. Box 52940
Tulsa, OK 74152

Art in America
575 Broadway
New York, NY 10012

Art Now
P.O. Box 219
Scotch Plains, NJ 07076

Art of the West
15612 Highway 7, #235
Minnetonka, MN 55345

Art Papers
P.O. Box 77348
Atlanta, GA 30357

Art Previews
1200 West 38th St.
Indianapolis, IN 46208

Art Week
12 South 1st St
San Jose, CA 95113

Artforum
65 Bleecker St.
New York, NY 10012

Artist's Magazine
1501 Dana Avenue
Cincinnati, OH 45207

ArtSource Quarterly
P.O. Box 369
Renaissance, CA 95962

ARTnews
48 West 38th St.
New York, NY 10018

Artscene
P.O. Box 97
Freeport, NY 11520

Artspeak
305 West 28th St., 13G
New York, NY 10001

Communication Arts
P.O. Box 10300
Palo Alto, CA 94303

Corporate Art News
48 West 38th St.
New York, NY 10018

Decor
408 Olive St.
St. Louis, MO 63102

Flash Art
1103 46th Ave.
Long Island City, NY 11101

Graphic Design: USA
120 E. 56th St.
New York, NY 10022

Illustrator
500 South 4th St.
Minneapolis, MN 55415

Museum News
1225 Eye St., NW, #200
Washington, D.C. 20005

Office Museum Directory
3004 Glenview Rd.
Wilmette, IL 60091

Southwest Art
P.O. Box 460535
Houston, TX 77056

US Art
12 South 6th St., #400
Minneapolis, MN 55402

Women Artist News
300 Riverside Dr., #8A
Grand Central Station
New York, NY 10025

Mailing Lists

Keeping a current mailing list of potential collectors, galleries, museums, institutions, and the like is an important aspect of your promotional plan. In addition to the people whom you come into contact within your daily activities, you can also add to your list through quality mail order data bases.

Art Networks
P.O. Box 369
Renaissance, CA 95962

Directory Marketing Association
230 Park Ave.
New York, NY 10017

NRPC Museum Mailing Lists
P.O. Box 12010
Des Moines, IA 50312

Media Directories

As you begin to contact the press, it is important for you to develop a good listing of contacts. The following guides will help you begin your search.

Magazine Industry Market Place
New York: R.R. Bowker

Media Personnel Directory
Detroit: Gales Research Co.

National Radio Publicity Directory
Peter Glenn Publications, Ltd.
17 East 48th St.
New York, NY 10017

Museum Directories

Targeting the right museums for your work is an important part of developing your career. Qualifying the venue before you present will save you time, money and frustration. The following publications will help you begin your search.

Art in America Annual Guide to Galleries, Museums and Artists
Art in America
575 Broadway
New York, NY 10012

American Art Directory
by R.R. Bowker
New York, NY

International Directory of the Arts
Wittborn Art Books, Inc.
1018 Madison Ave.
New York, NY 10021

Art Diary: The World's Art Directory
Milan, Italy: Giancardo Politi Editore
Flash Art
799 Broadway
New York, NY 10003

The Official Museum Directory
by The American Association of Museums
National Register Publishing Co.
1055 Thomas Jefferson St., NW
Washington, DC 20007

Photography

There are some basic guidelines to follow in photographing your works. The following references provide a good foundation for understanding how to produce a good photo.

Photographing Your Artwork: A Step-By-Step Guide Photographing to Taking High Quality Slides at an Affordable Price
by Russell Hart
Cincinnati: North Light Books
1507 Dana Ave.
Cincinnati, OH 45207

Photographing Your Artwork
by Russell Hart
Cincinnati: North Light Books
1507 Dana Ave.
Cincinnati, OH 45207
revised: 1987

Trade Shows/Art Fairs/Juried Competitions

Trade shows and art fairs are a good way for artists to sell their work directly to the public. A number of prestigious and exclusive art shows are held throughout the year. Juried competitions also expose your work to the public allowing it to be reviewed by critics, curators, art dealers, college professors, art organization directors and a variety of professionals from the community. The following guides will help you begin identifying and qualifying those fairs and competitions which are of interest to you.

Art Competition Handbook
by John M. Anglelini
Cincinnati: North Light Books
1507 Dana Ave.
Cincinnati, OH 45207
revised: 1986

Exhibition Directory
The Exhibit Planners
P.O. Box 55
Del Mar, NY 10254

National Calendar of Open Competitions
P.O. Box 433
South Whitley, IN 46787

Guidebook for Competitions & Commissions
Visual Arts Ontario
439 Wellington St.
Toronto, Ontario, Canada M5V 1E7

GLOSSARY OF TERMS

Academic: In reference to style of presentation, academic materials promote the importance of the art - the historical comparison of the art to other important works, and the significance of the artist's progression in development to the art world.

Archive: A complete record of all materials produced regarding your art and career including any and all printed materials depicting or discussing your work.

Artist's Proof: These prints are provided for the artist to verify color correctness and clarity. In most processes, artist proofs equate to 10% of the edition. The artist proofs are often signed "A-P" and numbered.

Artist Statement: A brief declaration by the artist describing their work, their philosophy, and from where they derive inspiration.

Body of Work: A group of works which are collectively represented as a single unit. Often, a body of works will have a theme or common thread which associates one to the other.

Chronological: Organization of items in date order.

Collector: A person who purchases a piece of art. Collectors often follow the career of artists in whom they are interested, purchasing a number of pieces over time.

Commercial: In reference to style of presentation, commercial materials promote the artist to generate revenues in contrast to academic materials which present the art. Commercial tools are often "glossy" sales tools.

Commercial Gallery: A commercial gallery is a place of business in which the sole purpose is to sell art for a profit. This type of venue usually focuses on selling a "product" versus those which promote the career of the artist.

Dealer: A person who deals in the sale of art. There are different types of dealers, often they are the owner or director of a gallery. Some dealers are independent and work in conjunction with the gallery dealer.

Exposure: The exhibition or showing of works of art for the viewing of person's other than the artist.

Gallery: A gallery is a place of business in which the primary purpose is to sell art for a profit. Some galleries work exclusively with "product" and others emphasize the development of the artist's career.

Hand-Touched: In reference to limited edition printing, the application of media or manipulation of the print by the artist. The artist has "touched" the work.

Institution: Venues which focus upon the academic value of artwork versus its economic value, including museums, universities, foundations, etc.

Patron: An individual who supports an institution such as a museum. Some patrons who purchase works for collections are known as collectors.

Philosophy: The artist's theories and beliefs which influence their creativity. Often thought of as the artist's reasons for making art. Some artist's do not have philosophies but work for aesthetic reasons.

Promotion: The process of publicizing artwork, artists or events. The purpose of promotion is to heighten the awareness and interest of the public in the artwork.

Publish: The process of producing a quantity of work based on the multiplication of a piece. These pieces are not copies but are usually original works unto themselves.

Retail: The price the public pays for a work of art.

Scholarship: In reference to artwork, writings which have been published about the artwork.

Strategies: The planned steps one takes in the development of their career.

Targets: The selected venues to which the artist's works will be presented. A good plan calls for researching the targeted venue for appropriateness to the work.

Teleresearch: The process of gathering information over the telephone; used to find and select appropriate targeted venues or individuals.

Venue: Any space which is used for the exhibition or sale of art.

Wholesale: The price paid by the gallery or middle-man who will in turn sell the work at a greater price to the public.

INDEX